Food Fights & Bedtime Battles

Food Fights & Bedtime Battles

A Working Parent's Guide to Negotiating Daily Power Struggles

TIM JORDAN, M.D.

B
BERKLEY BOOKS, NEW YORK

A Berkley Book
Published by The Berkley Publishing Group
A division of Penguin Putnam Inc.
375 Hudson Street
New York, New York 10014

This book is an original publication of The Berkley Publishing Group.

Copyright © 2001 by Tim Jordan, M.D.
Cover illustration by Seth Johnson and Annie Johnson
Text design by Tiffany Kukec

PRINTING HISTORY
Berkley trade paperback edition / July 2001

The Penguin Putnam Inc. World Wide Web site address is
www.penguinputnam.com

Library of Congress Cataloging-in-Publication Data
Jordan, Timothy J., 1954–
Food fights & bedtime battles : a working parent's guide to negotiating
daily power struggles / Tim Jordan.
p. cm.
Includes bibliographical references.
ISBN 0-425-17968-0
1. Child rearing. 2. Parenting. 3. Work and family. I. Title: Food fights
and bedtime battles. II. Title.
HQ769 .J768 2001
649'.1—dc21   2001029520

PRINTED IN THE UNITED STATES OF AMERICA
10 9 8 7 6 5 4 3 2 1

Contents

Contents

Introduction

"I DON'T WANT TO GO TO SCHOOL!!!" And with this salvo, the day begins for many parents. And this authority-challenging statement is just the first of many attempts by kids to engage their parents in those seemingly endless power struggles that play out all day long. *Food Fights and Bedtime Battles* is a book for any parent out there who has ever experienced firsthand a young child throwing a rip-roaring, earth-shattering, roof-raising tantrum during the wee hours of the morning or all the way through the last hours of the evening. And that should pretty much include most of us who have children. But, in particular, this book will address that group of parents known affectionately today as *working parents*, because they are at greater risk of being sucked into these recurring battles due to a number of reasons.

I have surveyed more than six hundred working parents (see sample survey, page x), and they all share many of the same concerns and face many of the same struggles with their children. Mornings are a nightmare in most homes as parents try to wake, dress, feed, and get the kids out the door and to day care or school. The after-work reunions are beset with whining, temper tantrums and power struggles as both parties attempt to make the transition from work and day care to home. And finally, the seemingly endless battles at bedtime, when parents are trying desperately to get the kids settled and asleep, are enough to make most throw up their hands in defeat. Each morning the alarm rings and the cycle repeats; not a very pretty picture, is it? And worse yet, the struggles at home carry over to the workplace. Parents report effects such as tardiness, feeling tired, frazzled, and distracted, work dissatisfaction, and a lack of self-confidence all as a result of their ineffectiveness in dealing with these parenting issues at home. Let's take a closer look at the survey results for a moment.

I asked parents three questions. The first question concerned what type of struggles they engaged in with their children. On average, they checked off at least two areas of concern, with the two most common being getting kids up, dressed and out the door (half checked this one) and power struggles over homework, bedtime, and television (half checked this one). Overall, 90 percent of parents indicated they experience at least one problem area in the mornings. And 85 percent have significant evening struggles with their kids over homework, television, and getting and keeping them in bed at night. Only about 20 percent of parents felt they had power struggles or tantrum problems with their children after school. My guess is that this number would be significantly higher if we were just surveying parents of 1- to 4-year-old preschoolers.

Question two gave working parents the chance to relate how parenting struggles were affecting their work performance. Parents on average checked off two areas each: with the most common being feeling frazzled, frustrated, guilty, angry, and drained on arrival at work, making it hard to get right to work (50 percent); and about 90 percent of working parents shared the common feelings of being frustrated, guilty, angry, tired, and drained due to parenting problems. And about half of these working parents felt their self-esteem suffered as a result of their parenting woes.

Finally, question three gave parents a chance to voice whether or not they'd like help and support in handling these significant power struggles with their children. Parents on average asked for help in two out of the three areas, the most common being how to be a more relaxed and confident parent who better delegated home responsibilities to their kids and spouses (75 percent). It's important to note that over half of all working parents in this survey asked for help in both areas concerning morning time and bedtime power struggles with their children.

Introduction

....

Survey given to more than six hundred working parents from more than ten states from 1995–1996.

Question 1: What kind of struggles do you have with your children that affects your job effectiveness?
On average, parents checked off at least two areas of concern:

- 90 percent of parents checked off problem areas in the morning, i.e., struggles around getting kids up, dressed, fed, and out the door, or power struggles in general.
- 85 percent of parents have significant evening struggles with their kids either around homework, TV, or getting and keeping them in bed.

Question 2: How does work performance suffer because of problems related to parenting?
On average, parents checked off two areas each:

- 50 percent of working parents experienced feeling frazzled, frustrated, guilty, angry, and drained upon arrival to work, making it difficult to get right to work.

- About 50 percent of parents felt their self-esteem suffered as a result of parenting problems.

Question 3: Would working parents like help handling these significant power struggles with their children?
On average, parents asked for help in two of the three areas listed:

- 75 percent of working parents wanted help in becoming a more relaxed and confident parent who better delegated responsibilities to their kids and spouse at home.
- Every area of help offered was checked off by more than 50 percent of parents surveyed.

....

Introduction

To be honest, these survey results didn't surprise me. I work with parents in many types of settings including office counseling, parenting and couple's communication classes, weekend personal growth retreats, and seminars and workshops around the country. And, I've not only heard their questions over and over again about these specific areas of parenting but also felt the emotions behind the questions. The feelings of frustration, inadequacy, and exhaustion are right there below the surface. And these feelings very quickly and easily come bubbling forth with very little prompting. So *Food Fights & Bedtime Battles* was written out of my direct experiences of what parents, and especially working parents, need and are asking for in terms of specific information and help to redirect these problems areas.

Now that we are more acutely aware of the problems working parents face, what to do about them? This book has been divided into three parts in order to approach these areas of concern from different perspectives. In Part I, parents will gain an understanding about why kids engage them in these struggles from a developmental perspective. This part of the book will include the normal developmental and behavioral "stages" that all kids go through, and in particular, the stages of autonomy and separation at eighteen to twenty-four months, the stage of identity and manipulation and boundary pushing at two to four years, and finally, the emotional growing-up stage at five to six years. The emotional unrest, ambivalence, and turmoil stirred up in kids as a result of these developmental "transitions" becomes the source of much of the friction and struggles between parent and child. Also included in Part I is an explanation of why parents get so frustrated, angry, and "plugged into" their children's mischief during these stages. It is through this deeper understanding of their child's and their own part in these struggles that parents can free themselves from their anger, guilt, and inadequate feelings to be more effective in their discipline.

Part II contains the practical solutions to both redirect and prevent the power struggles around these three important times of every family's day. Parents will learn how to stay detached, work out win-win agreements with kids concerning these areas, and then learn how to follow through in a kind, but firm, manner in order to ensure cooperation. All three problem areas, i.e., morning, after work, and bedtime power struggles, will be examined separately using a lot of real life examples from case histories, my counseling practice, and seminar participants. The "how-to" suggestions are presented in a simple, practical manner so that parents can quickly and easily put the information into practice with their own families. Parents being successful in these three areas will create many benefits both at home and in the workplace: mornings that run smoothly with a peaceful and warm good-bye scene; a fun, reconnecting time after work; more rested, confident, satisfied employees; feeling more balanced and at ease with their choices about working outside the home. Kids will experience the peace and security that comes from clear boundaries and the sense of calm in their home.

In Part III, the lessons learned through redirecting these three power struggle areas are summarized and generalized to give parents the long-term perspective of what this new model will mean for them and their children as the middle school and high school years approach. Pulling out of these battles and the peace and cooperation that follow go a long way in solidifying the relationship between parents and their children. If the relationship is trusting, safe, and loving, it becomes much easier to solve problems and create cooperative agreements with kids and then teenagers. And parents get a chance to practice detaching and letting go of these "minor struggles" in order to gain confidence in themselves and their children. By being able to stay detached while successfully redirecting these power struggles now, parents actually set the stage for the kind of relationship they will have with their children in the pre-teen and teen years. And this new model of problem solving will be effective in helping handle any area of conflict with children.

In Part III, I will also briefly touch on the effects of some other important factors in this process; e.g., factors such as separation, divorce, depressed parents, and ADHD/LD labels. And, I will also summarize the positive effects on parents' attitudes about work and their performance at work. Chapter 10 covers ten of the most common questions I hear from working parents. Parents will learn "What to do when . . ." about areas including working at home; working with grandparents, sitters, and teachers; sibling fights; homework hassles; desperate phone calls from home at work; separation issues; and how to take care of yourself.

Use the information in this book as it suits you and your children the best. Create success in your parenting, then pass this book along. But for now, let's get started on the developmental information.

Part 1

....

Awareness and Understanding

....

1

Ain't Misbehavin'!

One of the most important lessons I learned through working with renowned pediatrician Dr. T. Berry Brazelton was about the whole concept of "touchpoints." This concept teaches parents to:

- see the child's misbehavior through developmental eyes

- understand the effect of the child's current stage on why they are "acting up"

- become aware of all the gifts the child is receiving despite the turmoil of these stages

This "reframing" continues to be an integral part of my counseling work with families. It allows parents not to take the mischief personally and to stay more detached. In this calmer, more clear state of mind, parents are more likely to trust their gut and find creative ways to redirect their kids in ways that work for them.

So let's first look at the child's side of the story and then the parent's side concerning what goes on during some of these intense, tumultuous stages.

Child's Side of the Story

BURSTS OF LEARNING

A child's development occurs in bursts of learning. It is during these bursts that children will focus much of their attention and energy on one area of development (e.g., cognition, motor, language, etc.). While they are focusing on this area, the other areas of development tend to lag or regress.

For example, any children who at 10 to 12 months are saying a few words (bye-bye, Momma, Daddy) may suddenly stop speaking for a few months. That is because they have refocused their energy on learning to walk! They spend most of their day crawling, pulling up, falling down, and getting frustrated. Even after they've accomplished taking those first steps, words often don't reappear for a few months. It's as if they were saying to us, "This walking thing is soooo important to me right now, I'm going to be putting my heart and soul into it for now, so the other stuff like talking and using my hands is gonna be on the back burner for a while till I really get this walking thing down pat."

Once they've mastered their first steps, they happily

spend the next few months practicing and integrating their new skill; in this case walking, running, climbing stairs, etc. Then it will be time for another line of development to take center stage.

FALLING APART

Right before and during these bursts of learning, kids will often go through a period of regression or disruption, especially when they are going through one of the big, emotional, growing up, independence stages (18 months, 5–6 years, teenagers [see chapters 3, 4, and 5]). During these stages, kids are more moody and sensitive, out-of-sorts, have more fits and angry outbursts, seem more disorganized, have a harder time falling asleep, and wake up more in the middle of the night. It's almost as if they have to regress and become disorganized in order to gather up the energy and the focus for the "big learning" that is necessary for these big leaps in development.

TEMPERAMENTALLY SPEAKING

A child's temperament will play a large role in how intensely they "fall apart" during these important stages. Kids who are on the intense, bright, stubborn, determined end of the scale tend to bring a ton of energy and drama to these stages, whereas a child with an easier-going nature goes through the transitions more smoothly and quietly. So if you have a child who was colicky for their first four months and has been intense and demanding ever since, look out!

THE HAPPY ENDING

Mastering the challenges of each stage can be a tremendous opportunity for the child to enhance their self-confidence and sense of competence. It is a chance for kids to be able to say to themselves, "I did it!"

Remember the incredible smile and joy you see on a four month old's face when they are sitting on your lap, grab your fingers and pull themselves to a stand? Their legs lock tight and their face breaks out into that bright grin which says, "Look at me, I am so awesome!" Remember the first time your three year old pooped in the toilet and ran around gathering everyone to show off their prize? Or the first time they rode their two-wheel bike without training wheels? These are all chances to internalize that "It was tough work, but I did it all by myself." These victories are the building blocks that allow kids to feel capable and competent. It gives them the fuel to attack the next stage with confidence.

SUMMARY

So just before and during an important developmental stage, kids go through a period where they seem out-of-sorts. They become moody and irritable and throw more fits. In general, the more the disruption, the more important the learning is for the child. This regression serves a purpose as a way for the child to gather up steam and get their act together in order to successfully navigate the lessons for that stage. Once kids master the challenges of that stage, they experience the intrinsic joy that comes from these victories. So what looks like chaos and regression from the outside is actually the signal that "growing up" is soon to follow.

The Roller-coaster Ride:
The Parent's Side of the Story

PARALLEL LEARNING

What is fascinating to me is how much learning is going on with parents during each stage in a child's life. Parents have a chance to: learn from their mistakes and move on; not take things too personally (their kid's behavior, grades, etc.); be close and loving and detached at the same time; let go of control; set boundaries; get onto their child's wavelength and understand them at a very deep level; become aware of their own emotions that are stirred up by their children and why; and gain confidence in themselves as they effectively guide their children through each stage. In essence, parents are "growing up" side-by-side with their developing child.

"WHAT'S WRONG WITH MY CHILD?"

Unfortunately, parents often misunderstand and misinterpret all the disruptive behaviors their children display during the various stages. Parents see their child's behavior as abnormal and believe there is something wrong with their child. They also often see the disruption as a failure on their part; they take their child's regression personally. They wonder if it's the first signal of ADD (Attention Deficit Disorder) or hyperactivity or more serious psychological problems.

YOURS, MINE, AND OURS

All of this misunderstanding evokes a lot of emotions in parents; feelings of fear, anxiety, anger, guilt, confusion, frustration, disappointment, loss of control, inadequacy, defeat, and on and on. As a result of these feelings, parents tend to overreact, underreact, overpower, and come from a place of fear versus confidence. Thus, they add to an already overwhelming amount of emotion in the home produced by the child. Believe me, kids have more than they can handle of their own emotions. When you add the parent's intense feelings on top of that, you have a highly combustible mixture. This sets the stage in many homes for kids and parents to "lose it." Hence the negative press about the "terrible two's" and those "awful teen years."

"HERE WE GO AGAIN!"

So kids have a natural, normal, important roller coaster of emotions going up and down and up and down. If the parents misinterpret the goings-on and jump onboard with their own emotions, the two combined create overwhelming, unmanageable amounts of emotions and chaos. Instead of the stages with their associated disruptions coming and going in a normal fashion, they instead come and stay. Kids remain "stuck" in these stages for months and years creating the recurrent power struggles and scenes that cause families to come see me in my office counseling practice. Or cause parents to read every book on the market and attend every class and seminar on parenting, and generally feel like a complete failure as a parent. I bet a lot of you right now are dejectedly saying, "Been there, done that." So let's look at the bright side of the parent's side.

REFRAMING

If parents could reframe the stages and the associated behaviors as *normal* and *expected*, this would free them up to be more emotionally detached when dealing with their kids. Parents would thus be clearer about working out their own approach to the behaviors that fit their child. All the emotions can thus become fuel for learning about the child (and themselves), because it allows parents the opportunity to step back from the chaos and choose to look for the growth that is taking place. As a result, parents learn to understand their children at deeper levels; to reflect upon the child's past behavior and stages and what that can mean about the present phase; and to think about and wonder what all this means about who their child will become. Reframing allows parents to see, for example, that stubbornness at age three oftentimes translates into persistence and strong-mindedness in older kids and teens.

SUMMARY

I encourage parents to become aware of their own feelings, be a good observer of their child and his behavior at each stage of development, reframe the behaviors as normal, stay emotionally detached, and find some loving but firm ways to support their kids through their bursts of learning. This process will prepare parents for future stages and also the long-term process of letting go.

So the question for parents to ask themselves during these stages becomes: *"How can I be there for my child to support them through the challenges of this stage without add-*

ing my emotions to their already full mix, without doing it for them, and without getting in their way?"

As parents successfully navigate through the troubled waters of each stage, their confidence in their child's ability to get through the chaos and emerge more grown up or developed increases. What also increases is the parent's confidence in themselves as parents and in their ability to handle future stages.

PREVENTION IS THE BEST MEDICINE

If parents can anticipate the upcoming stages before they happen, then when the poop hits the fan they are ready for it. They understand what's going on and why their kids are acting out. It's much easier for them to stay detached and not take the regressions personally as their "failure." They can stay out of all the kid's emotions but still be there for them in a kind, loving, supportive, understanding way. Doesn't that sound a lot more reasonable?

Before we discuss the three most intense stages in early childhood, let's first talk about another concept, "Ghosts in the Nursery," which can have a huge impact on a parent's ability to effectively handle their children's stages.

2

......

Ghosts in the Nursery

When I see parents in my office who are plugged in to their child's mischief despite knowing that they should be doing otherwise, it's almost always because of a ghost in their nursery. Selma Fraiberg, author of *The Magic Years*, coined the phrase years ago to describe the phenomena whereby an adult brings experiences and beliefs and feelings from their past into parenthood. These can unconsciously resurface and haunt their parenting. Let me give an example of how this might look.

Mary was the mother of a rebellious six-year-old daughter, Holly, who, it seemed, was doing everything in her power to push her mom away. Mary told me, "I feel like I'm going through the teen years ten years early." When I asked Mary about her childhood, she explained tearfully that her mom was always depressed and distracted, and that her dad worked long hours, usually not arriving home at night until nine or ten. Mary was very upset as she described a childhood where she could never count on anyone being there for her. She then told me she remembered many evenings sitting in her room all alone, crying and saying to herself that "someday when I have kids of my own, I will *always* be there for them!" And she was, but she was overdoing it. When her six-year-old daughter tried to separate from her and have her own space or wanted to go to her friend's house, Mary had a hard time letting go and giving her the leash she needed, because some of her own old feelings would surface and cause her to get over involved, thus making Holly feel smothered. Holly would react by pushing her mom away through fits and mean words, causing Mary to feel unwanted all over again. This is how the "ghost in the nursery" works.

In my experience though, it is not just emotions and experiences from a parent's past that can turn into ghosts. It can also be any experience parents encounter in the pre-natal, pregnancy, perinatal, or postnatal period that produces feelings like sadness, worry, fear, or anxiety. These feelings tend to be put away below the surface so that we can move on with our lives and our parenting role. And these feelings tend to resurface during the turmoil and turbulence of developmental stages, causing parents to become over concerned, overreact, and parent from a place of fear and abnormality and ambivalence versus a place of understanding and confidence and love. These ghosts make it very difficult to parent in a detached, effective manner.

Common Ghosts in the Nursery and Their Effects on Parents

PARENTS' CHILDHOODS

People whose parents were absent, neglectful, depressed, and distracted tend to develop an attitude of: "*I'll be there for my kids!*" When parents feel that way, it's hard not to overdo for your kids, to smother them, to be over-involved in their lives. It is difficult to let go.

Parents who grew up in chaotic, alcoholic, unpredictable homes learned that they must be in control and have everything and everyone around them controlled/perfect, otherwise bad things might happen. They tend to avoid conflict; have a hard time staying out of their kids temper tantrums; have a tough time getting in sync with loud, different, emotional kids.

PRENATAL PERIOD

More and more couples today are facing problems with infertility. If parents have been through several years of waiting and testing and procedures and frustration, it sets them up to see their new baby as *a miracle child*, thus potentially paving the way for troubles being firm and setting appropriate boundaries.

14

RELATIONSHIP PROBLEMS

If there are problems in the relationship before or during the pregnancy, or if a couple gets pregnant unexpectedly and are forced to marry, it may set up resentments toward the child or competition and triangles between the parents and child. Some mothers unconsciously keep the fathers at a distance by criticizing their parenting, thus causing fathers to withdraw.

PERINATAL PERIOD

Any problems with Mom or the baby during the pregnancy can cause excess worry and concerns that carry over even after the baby is born normal and grows up healthy. Non-routine ultrasounds or seemingly trivial comments by doctors and nurses ("the baby's head seems a little small on the ultrasound, but I'm sure it's nothing") remain etched in some parents' brains forever even if everything comes out normal. This extra concern can cause over-parenting and overreaction to illnesses or normal childhood experiences while the child is growing up.

DELIVERY

Any problems with the delivery, especially when it threatens the health of the baby, can cause the parents to forever view their child with concern. Low Apgar scores, needing oxygen, requiring an emergency C-section, anything that violates a parent's expectation of a normal labor and delivery can cause emotions in parents that become ghosts.

POSTNATAL PERIOD

Any problems with the baby in those first months can again cause parents to forever see their child in a different light, with more worry and concern: babies born prematurely; babies hospitalized longer for jaundice or infections; babies with poor feeding and weight gain; babies who are hospitalized for infections/illness. A rough, worrisome start sometimes creates a lifetime of seeing that child through anxious eyes.

Let me give you a number of real-life examples from my practice of some ghosts in the nursery.

Sleeping

Kids who were preemies, siblings of kids who died from Sudden Infant Death Syndrome (SIDS), or kids with any postnatal problems such as seizures, apnea, infection, or "turned blue" are susceptible to sleeping problems.

Lisa brought her nine-month-old son, Randy, to see me, because he wasn't sleeping through the night. Lisa had had a history of endometriosis and, thus, infertility including three spontaneous miscarriages prior to finally becoming pregnant with Randy. The pregnancy was a nightmare because of first trimester spotting, numerous ultrasounds, and premature labor requiring bed rest during the final month of pregnancy. Randy arrived looking fine, but on the day of discharge he had a seizure, requiring another week of testing and observation. He went home taking medication and has never had another seizure. Lisa never got over the fear that something else bad was going to happen. And at nighttime her fears intensified (as they do for most parents) to the point where she had placed his crib alongside her bed so she could place her arm through the slats of the crib to keep her hand on Randy's back. She told me she did this so that "if he has a seizure and stopped breathing I'll be able to tell right away." So whenever Randy transitioned from his deep sleep to a lighter sleep and started fussing a bit and wiggling around, Lisa would wake up and pick him up and rock him. Thus the pattern was set for regular nighttime wakings.

Erica was the mother of 3-year-old Mariah who came to see me because Mariah was waking up two to three times a night and going into her parents' room to sleep with them. No one was getting enough rest and the parents were constantly arguing about the issue. Erica wanted Mariah to learn to stay in her own bed, but her resolve quickly evaporated in the middle of the night. When I asked Erica about her childhood, she got very quiet. Then she told me about how she had been molested by her stepdad as a little girl and no one stopped it for years, because they didn't believe her. She then made her own connection with how that experience related to Mariah. "You know, I wonder if I go in and take care of Mariah at nighttime because it's very important for me to protect her from feeling sad or hurt or alone. And maybe by protecting my daughter now it's a way for me to protect my little girl inside like I wasn't able to when I was growing up. Does that sound crazy to you?" And of course it didn't, because I understand the power behind these ghosts from our pasts.

Feeding

There are many children who are vulnerable to feeding problems. Babies who are born premature or small for gestational age (SGA); infants with slow weight gain; infants who failed at nursing especially if their moms were really committed to nursing; infants who are hospitalized for gastroenteritis (stomach flu) and subsequent weight loss. Anything that causes extra concern about weight gain, adequate nutrition, or the baby's size can become a ghost in the area of feeding.

*   *   *

During my fellowship training in Boston with Dr. Brazelton, I was called to the Chronic Care floor to consult on a fourteen-month-old girl who had been in the hospital for the past eleven months for treatment of Combined Auto Immune Deficiency Disease (CAIDD). During her second admission to the hospital for an infection at three months of age, her mom dropped her off and never came back. So Gretchen had grown up on the chronic-care floor and her two full-time nurses had become her substitute "parents." After an up-and-down course including some severe infections, a bone-marrow transplant and several setbacks that were near-death experiences, Gretchen had been healthy and growing for a few months. The nurses became concerned, however when Gretchen refused to let them feed her. They feared she might not continue her slow, but steady weight gain. Their fears about another possible infection and relapse and the thought that they might lose her were their ghosts. The ghosts didn't allow them to see that developmentally it was very important for Gretchen to start feeding herself as a sign of her blossoming autonomy. So the power struggle over feeding her was fueled by their fears.

Liz brought 4-year-old Dave into my office because of concerns about his picky diet. He was refusing to eat anything except what was on a small list of his favorite foods, which included macaroni and cheese, peanut butter, chips, cookies, and chocolate milk. Liz and Dave had been engaging in some major power struggles at mealtimes over the past three months with Dave usually winning out. When I asked about the pregnancy and perinatal period, Liz told me that Dave was only 5 pounds 2 ounces at birth despite being full term. He was very sleepy the first few months and a slow, picky eater. She gave up nursing after a few weeks because he seemed to prefer the bottle (despite her having gone to LaLeche League meetings for months to prepare herself). Slow weight gain required her to take Dave for weekly weight checks at the pediatrician's office. His feeding and weight gain picked up after about six weeks, but Liz could never really see him as normal or healthy. At four years of age Dave was in the middle of the growth charts for height and weight, yet Liz still saw him as being small for his age and underweight. And this extra concern was the fuel causing her to get overly upset about his normal picky-eating stage, which was her part in the recurrent power struggles at mealtimes.

Tantrums

Redirecting temper tantrums is tough for all parents, but especially so for parents with children who have been preemies, adopted, had perinatal problems, or who are/ were developmentally delayed for any reason.

*　　*　　*

Jenny was a 20-month-old active girl who was having frequent temper tantrums. Her parents were terrified of her
intense fits, and had tried everything to stop them, to no
avail. Jenny had been born two months premature but had
had a fairly uneventful nursery course lasting four weeks
primarily to get her weight up enough to go home. A routine
head ultrasound had revealed a grade I intraventricular
hemorrhage (IVH) which is common for preemies. The parents were told that most kids with a grade I IVH did fine,
although some ended up with mild learning problems or
ADHD, but they shouldn't worry about that now. Right! Jenny's parents couldn't forget about the possibility of these
future problems even though her first fifteen months went
very smoothly and Jenny was a good baby. But the concerns, the ghost, returned abruptly at about sixteen months
when Jenny started throwing herself on the ground with
blood-curdling screams over seemingly trivial matters. And
because of their ghost from the nursery, Jenny's parents
immediately jumped to the conclusion that this was the
first sign of ADHD. Out of fear, they tried desperately to
stop the fits with yelling, over control, and threats that
only seemed to make matters worse. Their frustration and
worries grew, causing them to become more impatient and
angry in their response to Jenny. All this caused Jenny's
tantrums to become more frequent, severe, and longer in
duration. So their overreaction to the tantrums was fueled
by their intense concerns about her future. They couldn't

see the tantrums as a normal reflection of her burgeoning autonomy because they had on ghost-tainted glasses.

Discipline/Setting Boundaries

Another area of parenting that is greatly affected by ghosts in the nursery is disciplining children. Setting boundaries can be tough when parents have a child who was a preemie, who was adopted, has a disability, a chronic disease (or a sibling with a chronic disease), or if there was a history of infertility before the pregnancy.

Mike and Mary had tried for five years to get pregnant, and had been through years of testing and procedures before finally becoming pregnant with Owen. They came into the office with Owen, now 3½ years, because in their words "we are being held hostage by our three year old!" It was obvious from Owen's office behavior that Mike and Mary were having a hard time setting appropriate boundaries with him. When I asked about the pregnancy history, Mary tearfully told their long story of infertility, how they had been on a five-year roller coaster of emotions ranging from hopeful to hopeless. After telling her story, Mary looked up at me and said, "You know, when we finally got pregnant we were ecstatic. And when Owen came out healthy and normal, we thought of him as our miracle baby." Then she stopped for a moment in reflection. "I wonder if that's why it's been so hard to say no to him and to follow through consistently with our discipline?" Bingo! She nailed the ghost right on its head.

Eitan was a 6-year-old boy referred to me because of behavior problems at home that were spilling over into school. He needed constant reminders and then some yelling and threatening before he would do his chores or get ready for school. Everyone, parents and teachers included, were frustrated by his unwillingness to follow directions or cooperate. Eitan's history revealed some developmental concerns including slow expressive language development and some mild language processing problems, which were being treated by a speech therapist. Eitan's dad, Dave, was especially frustrated because when there was something Eitan wanted, and they dangled it in front of him like a carrot, he could get organized and accomplish his task in no time. So he knew Eitan could do it. His wife, on the other hand, wasn't so sure he could understand and complete tasks, so she gave in to Eitan a lot and ended up doing a lot of things for him because "it was just easier." The ghost in the nursery for her was her ambivalence and confusion about how his language problems affected his ability to understand their discipline. And even though Eitan's speech therapist, teacher, and her husband were all totally clear he was more than capable of understanding directions and agreements, her uncertainty was felt by Eitan. And so he continued to push her buttons knowing he could usually get his mom to give in.

I hope it is becoming clear how powerful an influence ghosts in the nursery can be when it comes to interfering with parenting effectiveness. Sickness, premature birth, adoption, years of infertility, poor weight gain, disappointments about not being able to experience natural childbirth or breast feeding, and a disability or chronic illness (or a sibling with such), are all experiences that can create feelings in parents of uncertainty, worry, fear, and doubt. Often these feelings are pushed below the surface, but they tend to resurface when kids are going through stages that evoke emotions in their parents. These feelings then unconsciously tug on parents and influence how they handle situations. Let me share one other potential ghost shared by many parents today.

Working Parents

Statistics today reveal that 60–70 percent of mothers are out in the workforce in some capacity, whether part time or full-time. And many of these working moms have mixed feelings about being away from their kids all day and putting their kids in day care as early as 6 weeks of age. They experience feelings of sadness, confusion, ambivalence, guilt, anger, resentment, and inadequacy. They feel pulled in a million directions. Let's investigate these feelings a bit deeper.

• *Sadness:* Many parents experience a kind of grieving when they start their infants in day care. They miss their child. They feel sad whenever they miss out on any developmental gains ("She rolled over today for the first time!"). They might feel sad because they really want to stay home with the baby but can't afford to do it.

• *Guilt:* Very often people get messages from family, friends, or society that they *should* be home with their babies. If they were a "good mother" they'd stop being so selfish and self-centered and stay home. Or the guilt may come from within because *they* feel bad about having to leave their child in day care for eight to twelve hours a day.

• *Anger:* Many working parents get tired from trying to be the perfect worker and the perfect parent. So it's easy to get a little drained and crabby from burning the candle at both ends. And sometimes it's easier to express anger and blame others for not feeling good than it is to express feelings like sadness or fears or disappointment or hurt. Think about all the day-care staff who get blasted by angry parents over seemingly trivial matters.

• *Resentment:* Tired, crabby parents make for tired, crabby spouses. And if one spouse isn't pulling his or her share of the load at home with the housework or parenting, then it's fertile ground for resentment and finger-pointing and criticism. Some parents bring it on themselves because of being a martyr or because they like to be in control and have things done their way.

• *Inadequacy:* Remember my survey results from the introductory chapter? Lots of working parents feel like they can never find a healthy balance between home and work, leaving them feeling like they are failures in both places. And especially when they misinterpret their child's normal behavioral stages as abnormal or a negative reflection on their parenting (e.g., taking normal temper tantrums personally and blaming it on their rotten parenting skills).

• *Ambivalence:* All the above feelings cause many parents to feel ambivalent about their jobs and parenting. They feel torn between wanting to be home more and spend more quality time with their kids, yet they need to be investing more time and energy at work in order to create the income they want and the promotions and job satisfaction they desire.

So how do these feelings play out as ghosts? In my experience, they show up in several ways.

• *Overindulgence:* Many working parents who feel guilty and ambivalent about working outside the home have a hard time saying no to anything their child asks for—from candy at the check-out line to toys every time they go into any store or the mall. They can't say no to staying up just a little later to watch one more video or read one more book. Because these parents haven't been with their kids all day, they want their short time together in the evenings to be fun, and they don't want to see their kids unhappy at those times. So they give in a lot even when they know they shouldn't.

• *Loose Boundaries:* I see a lot of working parents having a hard time with setting boundaries or following through on agreements. There are a lot of scenes where the parents say, "No, no, no, no, no . . . fine, but next time you're going to bed at 8:00!" Kids can be very good at creating the right drama to pluck just the right heartstrings in their parents to get what they want:

"But I haven't seen you all day!"

"But I'm scared at nighttime."

I think of that TV commercial where the little girl with the busy mom says, "I wish I could be one of your customers." Think that mom wasn't a prime target to give in to almost anything!?!

And parents may think, "Well, I haven't been home much lately, and I miss my kids, so just for tonight I'll let them sleep in our bed." But, "just one night" becomes the rule instead of the exception. Then they become tired and crabby and resentful because they aren't sleeping well with the kids in their bed, their work performance is affected, which makes them feel even more out of control. . . You get the picture. And it's not a very pretty one either.

So let's move on to the next step in this process of achieving a healthy balance between home and work and in creating a more peaceful, cooperative environment. Next stop is understanding why our kids engage us in power struggles from a developmental perspective.

3

Playing the "Terrific Two's" (Ages 15-24 Months)

Toddlers in the "terrible two's" stage have gotten a pretty bad rap over the years. And the following scenario is the reason.

It is 7:30 A.M. at the Schulz house, and 2-year-old Charlie has just come down to the breakfast table.

"What do you want for breakfast honey, cereal or waffles?" asks his mom.

"I want cereal!" Charlie barks.

Mom dutifully pours in the cereal and the milk, and places the bowl in front of him. Charlie explodes.

"I don't want cereal! I want waffles!"

Mom, feeling a mixture of frustration, anger, and intimidation, hurries to remove the cereal bowl before it ends up on the floor. She then whips a frozen waffle into the toaster, and a minute later she gingerly places the trophy before the king.

"Here's your waffle, do you want syrup or jelly on it?"

And once again, Charlie explodes. "I don't want waffles! I want eggs!"

And with that said, Charlie throws his waffle onto the floor and starts to wail, banging his head on the highchair tray as only a two-year-old can. And Mom stands there looking totally defeated, wondering what she did wrong, and totally confused about what to say or do next. Does this scene sound familiar to anyone out there? I thought so. Let's talk a bit here to try to figure out why Charlie is acting this way and what to do about it besides throwing your own temper tantrum.

For the next three chapters, I'm going to discuss three important developmental/behavioral stages, which will help explain why kids get into the power struggles in the mornings, after work, and in the evenings. I'll break each chapter down into:

- Describe the important lessons the child is learning in that stage.

- Describe the feelings and disruptions that occur within kids as a result of going through the stage.

- Describe the feelings elicited in parents as a result of their child's emotional upheaval.

- Discuss how parents' reactions to their child's disruption can cause unhealthy cycles.

- Point out possible ghosts in the nursery that resurface at these stages.

- Discuss healthy and effective ways for parents to redirect and support their children through these stages.

So we will begin with the two year old's stage of autonomy.

Autonomy (Ages 15–24 Months)

LESSONS A CHILD LEARNS

Independence

Children somewhere in the middle of their second year start to assert themselves in many different areas. Having learned to walk has provided them with "wheels," and just like it will in their teen years, "wheels" means more mobility and thus more freedom to explore and satisfy their curiosities. This is the age when it becomes a major ordeal to change their diapers. Disagreeable toddlers will kick, fight, and do leg locks or whatever it takes to avoid those cold wet wipes. It becomes a major ordeal to get them in their car seats, or to get them dressed in the mornings. Isn't it amazing how they can be undressing themselves even as you are dressing them? Mealtimes become a nightmare of power struggles and picky eating and refusals to be fed. Their first words that come flying out of their mouths with a vengeance are NO! MINE! STOP! And if you have a child who is at the far end of the temperamental scale, scoring high on being intense, persistent, hardheaded, and demanding, look out! Because they will throw their heart and soul behind their blossoming independence.

Separation

With their new-found independence and mobility in hand, toddlers start to venture out more and more from behind our pants legs and skirts. This is the age when they start out at a family gathering clinging desperately to you on your lap, but when they hear their cousins' squeals of laughter from the next room, they slowly peel themselves off of you, slide to the floor, and slyly start to walk away from you. They'll look back a few times with that coy look that says, "Ha! I'm walking away from you and you can't stop me." They explore the next room for a few moments, then come bounding back into the room with an anxious look on their faces. And then they are back on your lap clinging for dear life. Once they get their sense of security and love back, they are off again to explore new horizons.

It's no accident that most toddler's favorite games are peek-a-boo type games. They love to be chased. I was playing with my 20-month-old godchild, John, a few weeks ago, and he kept hiding behind the couch, squeezing into this tiny spot between the couch and the wall. I'd start yelling, "John, where's John?" and I could hear him giggling away. I'd "find" him and with a roar, I'd pull him out and throw him on the couch and tickle him, then immediately he'd climb back over the edge of the couch to hide again. And they will keep up these hide-and-seek games for hours as a way to practice separation and independence.

Emotional Growing Up

The scene described above of separating from a parent at a family function is a good example to show how ambivalent toddlers are during this stage. One moment they want to grow up and separate more from their parents and be independent. The next moment they want to cling. They want to hide and they want to be caught. They want cereal and then they want eggs. This ambivalence creates a lot of turmoil within kids that often is expressed as temper tantrums, whining, and clinging behaviors. They seem out-of-sorts, more moody and demanding.

And this out-of-sorts behavior during the day carries over into the night, causing more wakings in the middle of the night. Lots of 18-month-olds who have slept through the night since three months of age are taken to their pediatricians because of these sudden night wakings. After their ears pass the exam for no infection, the wakings are often mistakenly explained as teething or back molars coming in.

It's usually just a symptom of a nervous system going through a critical period of development with the cost being some "emotional growing pains." These will resurface again during stages at five to seven years of age (see chapter 5) and during the teen years.

FEELINGS WITHIN A CHILD

As described above, kids during this stage experience many emotions, some conflicting. They get angry when they don't get their way or are made to do something they don't want to do (see diaper changes and car seats!). They have a lot of mixed feelings about the separation/independence deal, with part of them excited and curious to explore the world, and part of them a little anxious and insecure about it. They seem to want it all, and in the next breath not have a clue as to what they want. And in these moments of intense ambivalence, they blow a gasket and erupt into one of those rip-roaring, earth and ear shattering temper tantrums. And these tantrums can usually be turned on and off like a light switch if they get their way. Due to the eruption, parents are a basket case full of frustration, confusion, and anger, while seconds later their toddler goes off without a care in the world.

FEELINGS ELICITED IN PARENTS

• *Out of Control:* When kids get out of control and espe-cially with their intense anger, many parents feel panicky and helpless and out of control as well. And parents feel that they need to stop the tantrum. NOW!

• *Inadequacy:* Since we are so often powerless to stop the eruptions, we often feel like a failure as a parent: "If I was a good dad my son wouldn't be acting this way. And even if he was, I should be able to stop it." Our kids often pull their worst scenes out in public, so embarrassment creeps into the picture as well, further adding to our sense of failure.

• *Worries/Fears:* Many parents describe a reasonably happy, easy child who suddenly at age 18 months "turns into a monster!!!" "It was like Jekyl and Hyde" is a common phrase I hear in my office as parents describe their tod-dlers. Parents worry that maybe there is something wrong with their child. They ask themselves questions like:

"Is this the first sign of ADD or hyperactivity?"

"Is she angry with me because I'm back working part-time?"

"Is he going to be able to handle preschool? Grade school?"

"Is this going to ruin his chances for Harvard?"

"Is he going to end up like his uncle Vincent who was a hellion as a little kid and is now doing time for cocaine trafficking?"

Many parents let their fears do the walking and soon find themselves way out there with overblown ideas about what these tantrums will mean for their child.

• *Anger:* The child's intense, angry outbursts and demanding behavior stir up a lot of old baggage for many parents, including old unresolved anger. There is something about an assertive, demanding, tantrumming two year old that just makes us grit our teeth, put our hands on our hips, and want to let these little critters know who's boss around here.

PARENTS' REACTIONS

• *Getting Plugged In:* Because of all of their own intense emotions, parents end up getting too "plugged in to" or emotionally involved in their child's fits and emotions. The child has more than enough emotions of their own to deal with, so when parents add all of their feelings into the mix the system gets overloaded and overwhelmed. This then makes it more difficult for kids to deal with their own feelings, so instead of a stage coming and going in a normal fashion, it comes and stays. Which is why you have six year olds or twelve year olds still throwing fits to try to get their way.

• *Overreacting:* Many parents, especially ones who feel out of control, try to stop the tantrums through overpowering their child. They get very angry and frustrated and controlling, which only makes the tantrums more intense, more frequent, and longer-lasting.

• *Punitive:* Some parents react by becoming more punitive, by yelling or spanking or threatening or taking toys or privileges away. Usually this tactic tends to backfire, keeping everyone in the same cycle of frustration and anger. There are several reasons why it backfires. First, toddlers are supposed to lose it because they don't have internal self-control yet. So being angry at them won't help them learn it quicker. In addition, trying to negotiate with, bribe, punish or threaten a toddler when they are out of control is useless, because in those moments they are unable and unwilling to listen and they are "unreasonable." This will be true when they are age eight or sixteen as well. And again, it just adds to the already overwhelming anger and tension in the home.

• *Giving In:* Because of the intensity and persistence of some children, parents end up feeling drained and deflated and thus surrender to the child's demands. Their kids simply outlast them. For many parents, especially working parents (see chapter 2), it's just easier in the short run to give in and move on to the next event. They figure this is a way they can avoid the fits and the public scenes, so what's the problem with letting the kids win? Well, the problem in the long run is that they've created a monster, i.e., a child who thinks the world owes him a living; who has learned that the way for him to get what he wants in life is to be more obnoxious, aggressive, and overpowering. He believes that eventually he will get people to give in to his demands. He has also learned that his parents don't really mean what they say and, therefore, he doesn't need to respond to their requests right away and when he does it's worthwhile to put up a fight. This unhealthy pattern that the child plays out with his parents thus can carry over to his relationships with other adults like teachers, coaches, grandparents, and sitters.

GHOSTS IN THE NURSERY

• In chapter 2 I gave the example of the child who was born prematurely and whose parents were concerned that the tantrums were an early indicator of ADHD. I remember seeing another ex-preemie, 2-year-old Billy, in a follow-up clinic who was having frequent, intense fits. His parents were way too involved in the tantrums despite knowing better. His intensive-care nursery experience included a head ultrasound that revealed a Grade II intraventicular hemorrhage. Like Jenny in chapter 2, Billy's parents were read the riot act about potential future problems due to the bleed. So when little Billy started throwing himself around during his fits and banging his head on the floor, his parents immediately panicked, thinking that he might cause a re-bleed in his head. Thus, they would do anything to stop the tantrums for fear of what they might cause.

It is common to see parents who had sick babies, small for gestation age babies, or premature nursery graduates overreact to tantrums.

• *Parents with Emotional Baggage:* Some people come to parenthood with past baggage from their own childhood due to having felt rejected or abandoned by their own parents. These parents are needy for love and attention. New babies are one place they can pour their love into and for the first year and a half get love and smiles in return. But when the toddler starts to separate, pull away, become more independent and need the parent less, feelings of rejection are triggered and these parents have a hard time letting their kids go off into the world and explore. They tend to be more smothering and anxious, which carries over to their kids, causing them to feel more anxious and insecure or rebellious.

• *Parents with Poor Self-confidence:* These parents are especially vulnerable to overreacting to their toddler's mischief and especially when they are out in public. It's hard to stay calm and detached if you are fearful and anxious about everyone's judgments. You have to be pretty confident in yourself to stay the course and use your effective tools when being stared at by judgmental onlookers.

• *Parents with Chaotic Childhoods:* Parents who grew up in homes where there was a lot of yelling, anger, raging, alcohol abuse or physical or verbal abuse often have a hard time when situations feel out of control or when there is conflict or anger in the air. When their toddlers throw a fit these parents experience a strong urge to stop the chaos, causing them to get too involved in the tantrums.

HEALTHY/EFFECTIVE RESPONSES TO
THE AUTONOMY STAGE

• *Understand the Stage for What It Is:* Parents need to understand the importance of the learning behind their child's need for autonomy and separation. It is at this stage that children are supposed to learn that the world is a safe, exciting place to explore and learn from. They learn that they can become more independent and master challenges on their own. And with this exploration and mastery comes self-confidence, self motivation, and self awareness. Parents need to remember that the ambivalence within the child about this emotional growing-up stage is causing most of the fits. And this behavior is normal and expected especially if the child has a more intense, stubborn, independent temperament.

• *Stay Detached:* From this understanding, it is much easier to stay detached; not take their tantrums personally; not blame yourself; not worry that your child is abnormal; not allow yourself to get frustrated or angry or "plugged in;" keep your emotions out of it.

• *Value Exploration/Be There When They Return:* It is important that kids feel free and excited about toddling off to explore their world. It's very unhealthy for them to take on their parents' anxieties and fears about separation. It's our job as parents to prevent accidents by child-proofing their environment. Then gladly, with confidence, send them out to satisfy their curiosities. It is equally important for you also to be there for them when they return with their treasures and stories and bumps and bruises. Lovingly and warmly welcome them back with smiles and hugs and questions about "so what were you doing?" Even if they can't talk, this warm home base refuels their sense of security, which allows them to head back out there for more adventures and more learning. It is important for a child to know that he has safe people to return to for support and nurturing and to share his adventures with. Kids need to be allowed to make some mistakes and fall down and get some bumps out in the world as part of their learning process. Parents can take this opportunity to let go a little and let their kids grow up, thus preparing them for the big letting go's of the teen years.

• *Follow Through with Actions and Few Words:* My wife, Anne, and I were out in our front yard raking leaves one day with our 15-month-old son, John. He was playing on the sidewalk, and at one point he started to walk into the street. We immediately went over and escorted him back onto the yard with the words, "John, you need to play in the yard." Well John, being the true-blue toddler that he was, stared back into our faces and walked right back into the street. Again, we went right to him saying, "John, you need to stay in the yard. If you walk in the street, we'll have to take you inside and you won't be able to play out here." At this point John hesitated, stared at the street, then back at us, then indignantly walked toward the street. Anne immediately picked him up and carried him (kicking and screaming) inside the front door, telling him gently that "we're not willing for you to play in the street. As soon as you can calm yourself down, we'll try again." John hollered at us from behind the glass door for a few minutes. Once he had settled, we brought him back out and told him to play in the yard.

And of course he didn't. He took off for the street with a bang, so we once again carried him back into the house, while he wailed furiously. We told him that as soon as he could calm down, we'd let him come out as long as he stayed in the yard. It took him more than ten minutes to chill out this time, but when we brought him back out he had gotten the message. He played happily in the yard, and even helped us as only 15-month-olds can.

Kids at this age need immediate, kind-but-firm boundaries, and actions that speak louder than words. I see too many parents today flapping their gums way too much with their toddlers, then not following through. It usually takes some repetition, but even toddlers can learn that you mean what you say and that you are not going to get sucked into their tantrums.

• *As Soon As . . . :* This is also the age when parents hit a fork in the road. One choice is to use dominance to get your child under control or to cooperate. The other choice is to learn to set a boundary, disengage from any potential power struggle, but follow through in a kind-but-firm manner. Let me clarify further with another example from our home.

When our John was 18 months old, he started fighting us in the mornings about changing his diaper. He'd kick and scream and lock his legs tightly in some yet unnamed WWF maneuver. We could have chosen to manhandle him, with two of us holding down his arms and unlocking his legs to somehow manage to overpower the wet diaper off and put a dry one on. We chose not to go down that path because we knew if we did we'd have to use these tactics five times a day and that would become our pattern for gaining cooperation.

Instead, we chose an alternative route. We decided that the order of his morning would be to get up, change his diaper, get dressed, go down for breakfast, then start the day's activities. He was still too young and didn't have the verbal ability to have an opinion on the order of his mornings. So when he balked at having his diaper changed and started screaming, we told him in a loving but firm voice that we weren't willing to fight him, and that, "*As soon as* we can change your diaper and get you dressed, we'll be ready to go down for breakfast. Let us know when you're ready." Then we turned and walked out of his room leaving him literally bouncing off the walls in anger. We checked back in with him every five to ten minutes, asking him if he was ready to change his diaper.

"NO!" was the answer, so we'd calmly repeat, "As soon as you're ready to get it changed, let us know." Then we'd return to our bedroom. This went on the first couple days for thirty to forty minutes before he'd begrudgingly let us change him. Then it was only fifteen to twenty minutes for a few days, then ten minutes. Until one day, honest to God, he walked into our bedroom just minutes after round one with a diaper in his hand and told us, "I'm weddy now." And though it had taken us close to a week of training, we were essentially done with power struggles around diaper changes. It was well worth the time it took up front to teach him that we meant what we said, and that we were going to follow through with the order of the day without any games. Those magical words "as soon as" can be very powerful for kids at this stage. For working parents who are reading this and saying, "I don't have thirty to forty minutes in our mornings to do this," I want to reassure you that *yes you do*. And even stronger, you'd better take the time now to handle these power struggles because they are only going to get tougher to redirect with each passing month. Allow yourself extra time in the mornings if you are in the middle of working through such an issue. Wake up thirty minutes early until you've gotten over the hump, then go back to your regular routine. Teaching kids about boundaries takes some time and patience. There is no easy way around it. You have to invest some time and energy for these invaluable lessons. Do whatever you need to do to create the time, then you're done with it. And remember that we're not talking about six months worth of horrendous mornings, we're talking a handful, and then it's a nonissue. It truly is worth the effort in the short-term for a long-term gain in cooperation.

• *Don't Walk Away, Renee . . . ?:* Often times the best thing you can do when a toddler flips out into a temper tantrum is to walk away, giving the behavior as little energy as possible. How you walk away is important though. If you walk away angry and frustrated after yelling at or disrespecting the child, the message is: "I'm mad at you for being two, for doing what you're supposed to be doing at your age, and what you are doing is bad, and therefore I'm withdrawing my love." This can feel like rejection or abandonment to a child.

If, on the other hand, you remain calm and detached but still loving and caring as you walk away, what you are saying is: "I love you, and I'm not willing to be hit or kicked or spit at or have things thrown at me. It's OK to lose it when you are two. I understand, and I'm not willing to get sucked into the drama. I'm not willing to allow your roller coaster of emotions to cause me to lose my cool and then add my emotions to the mix. As soon as you are calmed down, we can be together again." Now obviously you don't actually say all of that, but your actions do convey that message. And as most of us with two year olds have discovered, when you walk away and remove any audience participation, the tantrums typically resolve quickly.

So what this could look like for you, when your toddler has lost it and is screaming and lashing out at you is the following. "I understand you are mad, and I'm not willing to be hit or kicked, so as soon as you can calm down and stop hitting, you can come be with me." Keep the talking short but to the point with a kind-but-firm tone. You'll be surprised at how effective it is.

For some children, if you catch them early on in a fit,

you can put them on your lap, hug them while gently talking to them, and this allows them to settle down. But for most kids, this tactic would make them madder and result in them trying to hit, kick, or bite. So you'd be better off with the previous maneuvers. You know your child, so trust yourself as far as which way would work best for your child.

• *Choices, Choices, and More Choices . . .:* It does help to give your toddler choices. Remember that they understand lots more than they can express. The choices at this age are simple ones: do you want to wear this shirt or that one? Do you want milk or juice? They'll grunt or point and then feel very powerful, which allows them to settle down a bit. Don't overwhelm them with choices though, because we've already learned how quickly toddlers can get into overload. We'll talk more about how to give kids lots of appropriate power in the next chapter.

I hope these suggestions will help you to understand and more effectively redirect your toddlers. It's a fascinating and important stage for them. And the potential lessons to be learned are obviously essential for a child being able to grow up feeling loved, secure, and powerful. Let's move on now to the next important stage of identity.

4

....

"We're Being Held Hostage by Our Three-Year-Old!" (Ages 2-4 Years)

P reschool-aged kids are *so* fascinating, and they can also be a handful for parents. There is a tremendous amount of learning packed into these preschool years. But first let me give you an example addressing the challenging part.

It's Friday night and the family decides to go out to dinner together.

"Let's go out for pizza" suggests seven-year-old Mariah.

"I don't want pizza!" barks 3½-year-old Tyler. "I want a cheeseburger."

"I don't want to go to a hamburger place this time. We've gone there the last five times. It's not fair," complains Mariah.

"Tyler, she's right. It's her turn to pick," says Mom.

"I don't want pizza, I'm not going!" screams Tyler, as his tantrum begins to unravel.

"Honey, it's not fair to your sister. We'll go for burgers next time." Dad is almost pleading at this point.

At this point, Tyler is screaming and kicking and writhing around on the floor. And from past experience everyone knows he will keep it up unless something happens.

"Actually, I don't really care," offers Mariah. "We can go for hamburgers."

"Are you sure honey?" asks the relieved mom.

"Yeah, it's fine with me. I'm hungry."

"OK, Tyler, we'll go for burgers tonight, but *next* time it'll be Mariah's turn to choose," Dad musters, trying to save face and act like they haven't been defeated—again. And magically, Tyler's tantrum switches to a sly grin that says, "I gotcha—again." And the family rides off into the sunset with Mom and Dad feeling defeated and powerless. They've won the battle, but are losing the war. They will pat Mariah on the back and give her strokes for being so cooperative and so good. Which gives her a short-term good feeling, but a bigger, and fast-building resentment about having to give up what she wants all the time. Which translates for many people into a lifelong pattern of giving in and giving up your desires and feeling resentful, angry, and bitter (toward spouses, bosses, family members, co-workers, their own kids someday).

I can't tell you how many parents of 3-year-olds have come to my office counseling practice with the following complaint: *"We are being held hostage by our three year old!!!"* Preschoolers are *very* powerful little creatures, and that power can either be channeled into appropriate ways or it can create major power struggles and chaos. Let's talk first about the child's part of the stage, and then we'll tackle the parent's part.

LESSONS A CHILD LEARNS

Many people call this age the Stage of Identity, which contains many important lessons for kids to learn. Here are the highlights:

• *Boundaries:* What is your space, and what is mine? Where do I stop and you start? When do I cross the line and get into your space? What are my limits? How far can I push where it's still okay? What is appropriate behavior and what is not?

• *Socialization:* Kids during these years move from parallel play to more rich, interactive play which includes more and more language. They learn to share, ask for what they want, be assertive, be empathetic, handle conflicts with words versus aggression.

• *Power:* How much power and say-so do I have in my life? How much control do I have? How can I be powerful without overpowering others? How can I feel a sense of control without being too bossy or controlling? How can I make a difference and be helpful and valuable?

• *Egocentric:* The world and everyone in it does and should evolve around me and my needs, shouldn't it? Like the teen years, preschoolers get very concerned about themselves. A cut with a drop of blood creates wailing and high drama. They bark commands and expect immediate gratification. They masturbate and become curious about how they look compared to others. They try out all kinds of different roles; one moment they are growling like a tiger, then they are gentle as a lamb. They become monsters, Power Rangers, Barney all in the same day. Little boys walk around in mommy's high heels with her purse slung over their shoulder. I have a picture of my son, T.J. at three years of age standing in front of a full length mirror staring at himself, wearing only a cowboy hat, cowboy boots, and a holster. Children at this stage show the full range of emotions, and can go from totally happy to totally berserk in a blink of an eye. And over time they internalize all these experiences and the feedback they've gotten about themselves from parents and other adults and decide who they are. They learn which parts of themselves are approved of, and which parts they need to tuck away. So by the time they enter school they've made a lot of decisions about who they are and how they fit in.

• *Aggression:* How do I channel my energy and aggressive feelings in appropriate, healthy ways? How can I be assertive but not blow people away? How can I handle my impulses and develop self-control?

• *Fears:* How can I learn to face and handle my own fears? Fears of the dark, monsters, bees, loud noises, sirens, etc. How can I use my imagination and fantasy play and aggression to handle my fears?

These are the most important lessons kids learn at this stage. And much of the learning occurs through these means: teasing, pushing boundaries, manipulating, debating, arguing, and engaging people in power struggles.

In particular, they learn a lot about power, control, and boundaries through these maneuvers. And they bring much *drama* to this age as well that can look like whining, complaining, and fits as well as intense joy and total body laughter. And of course, a child's temperament again plays a large role in how intensely they act and push.

FEELINGS ELICITED IN PARENTS

Because of the above-mentioned behavior from their preschoolers, parents often feel:

• *Provoked:* Because their authority is threatened. As a result, they feel like they have to show the child who is boss.

• *Manipulated:* And then, as a result, resentful and angry (remember the hostages).

• *Out of Control:* Because their child is intensely out of control.

• *Drained and Defeated:* Especially if they've been worn down by a highly intense, stubborn, persistent child.

• *Fearful:* That their child is becoming a spoiled brat who will never have any friends and will someday end up in prison or on drugs.

PARENT'S REACTIONS

• *Power Struggles* Because kids this age are so powerful and persistent, many parents get sucked into tons of arduous arguments and debates or they get engaged in intense power struggles. They are good at provoking their parents, and when parents feel that their authority is being threatened, it's hard for them to not grit their teeth and show them who's boss. When we get sucked into that state of mind, we are essentially playing into their hands. Because whenever a little kid can get a big kid, i.e., their parent, locked into mortal combat (a power struggle), it gives them a tremendous sense of power and control—an inappropriate kind of control—but when you are three years old you'll take your control however you can get it.

And parents who like to be right, and who like to be in control will be especially vulnerable for getting into tug-of-wars and arguments. Verbal, intense four year olds are the best debaters I know, and they always have a last word or excuse to throw into the mix. And some parents just can't let it go either, and so power games rule in those homes.

• *Family Feud:* Many parents also get into some unhealthy patterns with uncooperative preschoolers that involve reminding, nagging, coaxing, pleading, begging, scolding, yelling, threatening, punishing, spanking, and bribing. Some parents can even manage to use all of these tools in a twenty minute power struggle. These efforts might gain you a momentary, short-term win, but you've created more long-term headaches because you'll have to resort to these same tiresome maneuvers the next time you want cooperation. It becomes like the family play, where everyone has their own role and their own script. No one really likes this kind of drama, but it has become the way the family operates over time, and it's a hard habit to break.

• *Giving In:* Many parents today, especially in families where both parents work, are guilty of this one. It's hard to stay kind and firm when you are exhausted. Persistent kids sometimes just outlast their parents. It becomes a "no, no, no, I said NO!, no . . . fine, but only for this time . . ." But just for this time often becomes the rule instead of the exception. And preschoolers can spot a wishy-washy adult a mile away, and that's the person they will push limits with the most.

This reminds me of the story of the little girl who was out in the yard playing one day when her mom called out, "Annie, time to come in for dinner!" No response. A short time later her mom called out, "Annie, time for dinner. Come on in!" Again no response. Finally, her mom shouted out angrily, "Annie, come in for dinner right now!" Whereupon the little girl came inside, ran into the kitchen, and with an innocent look on her face said, "Sorry Mom, I didn't hear you when you called me the first two times."

When parents give in and don't follow through, kids never learn that parents mean what they say. They become parent-deaf, which later turns into teacher-deaf and coach-deaf and spouse-deaf. They don't respond to a request until there have been eight of them with increasing volume, ending in a yell and *then* they do what they've been asked. Maybe. But the parent usually feels bad because they don't like to yell at their kids, and they also feel upset with themselves because they realize they got sucked into the unhealthy pattern again. It's also a draining way to parent. These struggles leave parents feeling exhausted and frustrated and inadequate.

- *"Mommy, I Can't!":* Some preschoolers also display what my friend Kath Kvols, author of the book *Redirecting Children's Behavior*, calls "Cower Power." They are such experts at whining and "I can'ts" that their parents end up doing a lot of things for them that they could or should be doing for themselves.

Kate was the mother of powerful little 5-year-old Molly, who was an authority on cower power. Mornings had become a nightmare, trying to get Molly up and dressed. Kate would have to wake her three or four times before Molly would finally arise from her throne. Once up, the dressing issue came to the forefront.

"I don't want to get dressed. I want to stay home today," Molly whined.

"Honey, you can't miss kindergarten. Don't you want to play with your friends at recess?" Mom's coaxing had already kicked into gear.

"Will you dress me?" Ah, here we go again.

"Honey, I'm busy right now and you're old enough to

dress yourself." At this point Kate's voice is becoming as whiny as her daughter's.

"But I can't! These buttons are too hard," wails Molly.

"Honey, *please* just get yourself dressed this morning. Mommy's busy, and I know you can do it. You did it last Sunday before your recital," pleads Mom.

"But I can't Mommy, I'm too tired. Pleeeeease!"

After about twenty minutes of this dance, Kate throws in the towel. "Come here. We're going to be late for school again if you don't get dressed now. But this is the last time I'm doing this for you. You're too old for me to be dressing you like this." Despite having given in, Kate is doing her best to not lose face and to put on a stern front.

"Okay Mommy," says a triumphant Molly, sporting that coy little grin that just screams out, "Yesssss!!!"

And, of course, tomorrow morning will be no different, nor the weeks or months afterward until Kate becomes aware of the pattern and her part in it.

• *In the Long Run . . . :* Bribing, punishing, yelling, overpowering, and giving in are short-term relief with a long-term cost. Parents like Kate tell me that it's just "easier in the moment," which is probably true. Most working parents I know are guilty of that logic. But in the next breath they'll also realize that "I think we've created a monster." A monster that has learned that "I can outlast my parents enough of the time that it's worth pushing the limits most of the time, because I'll probably get my way." A monster that's learned her parents don't mean what they say; that, "I don't need to respond to requests the first time because they'll come back and remind me ten times anyway before they really mean it (yelling); that the way for me to get what I want is to throw a fit and escalate my mischief because enough of the time my parents give in and give me what I want. And even if they don't, it's still worth the price of admission because I get a tremendous sense of control by creating all this fuss and chaos. I push buttons and people jump. Even if I get yelled at and sent to my room, I still like that sense of control I get from these scenes." And that is Identity Stage logic at its best.

GHOSTS IN THE NURSERY

• *Miracle Babies:* Whenever parents see their child as extra special, a "miracle baby" if you will, because of a history of infertility, problem pregnancies, rough deliveries, prematurity requiring intensive care, etc., these parents become vulnerable to giving in much of the time. (Remember the story of Mary and Mike and their ghost in the nursery from chapter 2.)

• *Working Parents:* Any parent who feels guilty about not spending enough time with their children is vulnerable to giving in too much. You want your evenings to be fun quality time, so it's easier to give them what they want as opposed to dealing with unhappy, fussy kids. Plus, most working parents are tired at the end of the day; their patience level and frustration tolerance are low. And, their resolve is low. So they are set up for the patterns described earlier such as reminding, yelling, pleading, and bribing. They are an easy target for power-hungry kids looking to engage someone in a power struggle. Out-of-balance working parents who feel out of control in their lives (internally) may seek some semblance of control externally by being too controlling with their kids. Perfectionism about a clean house and perfect table manners can lead to unnecessary power struggles in those areas. "If I can just get my kids under control, maybe the rest of my life will follow suit," is the unconscious reasoning. But these parents end up more often than not with arguments and tug-of-wars instead of the control they wanted.

• *Kids with Disabilities/Developmental Delays:* One cause of parental ambivalence in discipline comes from parents not being sure if their kids understand the disciplining. They aren't clear if their child with ADHD, Language Delay, or Down's syndrome really understands their directions, limits, and directives. And so they enter discipline situations unclear and wishy-washy versus clear and firm. We all know from experience that preschoolers have sensitive radar able to spot ambivalent parents a mile away. And that's the one they'll push and tease and manipulate.

• *All in the Family:* If parents have someone in their family who is a black sheep, it can set them up to overreact to their preschooler's behavior. They may have experienced the pain resulting from a parent or sibling with mental illness, alcoholism or drug addictions, school problems from Learning Disabilities (LD) or ADHD, or trouble with the law. So when their 3-year-old gets into some major raging and out-of-control behavior, the parents will want to stop it now, or it might end up leading to what their relative went through (jail, addiction, unemployment, drop out). These parents are thus often too controlling, too quick to anger, too quick to overpower or punish. And so the unhealthy cycles begin.

HEALTHY, EFFECTIVE PARENTING FOR THE STAGE OF IDENTITY

• *Understand This:* First of all, understand that it is a 3-year-old's JOB to tease, push limits, and be egocentric and manipulative. It is their God-given right, it is normal, and it is essential for their learning the lessons they need to learn. Therefore, it is not the parent's job to stop this behavior from happening, but instead to redirect *themselves* such that they don't get too emotionally involved in all the drama. It's our job to redirect the energy to more useful channels, not to engage it or get frustrated with it.

• *Act Immediately!:* Remember that actions speak louder than words. Recall our adventure with John and his morning diaper. Learn to take action immediately as opposed to repeating a command five times or threatening without following through. If your two-and-a-half-year-old hits you, immediately tell him in a firm voice, "That hurts. I'm not willing to be hit. As soon as you can play without hurting, come find me." And then walk away, even if they flip out. Immediate action like this registers in their heads that you mean what you say and inappropriate behavior won't be tolerated. And this is one of the ways that you teach kids about respect, preventing later problems with issues like mouthing off.

• *Agreement and Accountability:* Once your toddler has fairly strong expressive language, you can begin to implement a model for gaining cooperation that will take you successfully through the teen years. I suggest to parents that they think in terms of agreements and accountability versus rules and punishments. And that would look like the following:

Find a quiet, relaxed time when there is no mischief going on in order to address an issue. Family meetings are the best place for this because you've already set those up as the regular weekly place to handle issues and you have a successful process in place. See *Keeping Your Kids Grounded When You're Flying by the Seat of Your Pants*, by Tim Jordan, M.D., and Sally Rains, 1999, for more extensive discussion on how to set up family meetings.

Own your part in the issue. You can say something like, "I've been nagging you a lot about getting ready in the morning, and yelling too. I don't like to start off our day like that, and I bet you don't either. So let's talk about mornings together and come up with a plan that works for both of us. How do you think our mornings should look?"

Talk it through till you come up with an agreement that works for both of you. But *listen* mostly, and use the kid's ideas as much as you can, within reason. The more say-so they have in the final solution, the greater the sense of ownership they have; and thus more cooperation follows.

Take as much time as you need up front to make sure everyone is *really* clear about the agreement and about how you will follow through. Those extra few minutes spent making sure everyone is in agreement and clear will save you a lot of unnecessary fuss in the future.

Ginny and her 16-year-old daughter Darci were in my office because they were at each other's throat constantly. Ginny said she couldn't trust Darci because she had gone back on too many agreements. The Sunday before, Darci had asked to go to her friend's house to study for a few hours. It was 6 P.M., so Mom said, "Fine, just be home by 8 P.M., and before you go, clean up your room like you said you would Friday!" So Darci cleaned up her room, and left to study. Sure enough, 8:00, no Darci. 8:10, no Darci. At 8:20 Darci strolls nonchalantly into the house and Ginny was furious. "You told me you would be back by 8:00, it's 8:20 and once again you broke our agreement!" Darci couldn't believe it. "Now wait a minute, you told me I could be back at 8:00, that was two hours to study, but you made me clean my room first and that took twenty minutes, so I didn't leave till 6:20, so I assumed I didn't have to be home until 8:20."

Get the idea now about how valuable it would have been for the mom and the daughter to spend an extra minute to get *crystal clear* about their agreement? Both were right from where they sat. So take the extra moments up front to avoid hassles down the road. Here is an example of how that would look with a 5-year-old. Let's continue on with the discussion above about mornings.

"I want you to wake me up in the morning," offered 5-year-old Billy.

"I can do that," replied Mom. "Would you rather put your clothes out the night before or choose them in the morning?"

"I like putting them out the night before."

"Great! What should we do about watching television in the morning before school?"

"I don't think we should watch television in the morning, because it's not fair that Johnny [2-year-old brother] can watch it while I'm getting dressed and eating breakfast."

"That sounds reasonable to me. How about this idea. After I wake you up, you can get dressed and get your schoolbag packed. Then you can come downstairs and eat breakfast. And if there is time left over before the bus comes, we can read a book together. Would that work for you?" asked Mom.

"Yes!" said Billy excitedly. "I like reading books in the morning."

"Well, good then. Let's see how our new plan works this week. Thanks for sharing so much."

• *Stay in Charge . . . of Yourself!:* Kids in this 2–5 year-old age group love a good tug-of-war with adults because it gives them a tremendous sense of control and power. So it is vital that parents stay calm and keep their emotions (frustration and anger especially) out of the equation. As mentioned previously, kids bring more than enough of their own emotions that they are trying to deal with and handle to this stage. Adding our emotions to the mix makes it an overwhelming proposition for them, and raises the stakes to an unmanageable level. We need to stay loving and present, but at the same time keep our emotions out of it, i.e., stay emotionally detached.

• *Give Power!:* The best medicine for kids at this age is to give them more appropriate power, control, and say-so in their lives, *preventatively*. One of the main reasons they engage us in power struggles is to feel a sense of power and control. So give it to them preventatively—in large dosages. Because when they feel powerful, they don't need to engage us in these battles. They already feel powerful and in control; and thus you can avoid most of the power struggles.

The following are some examples of how to empower preschoolers:

• *Give Choices:* This is a common, obvious example but a good one. As long as the choices are all okay with you, go for it. Let your children choose what clothes to wear, what to eat for breakfast, who puts on their seat belt (not *if* they put it on), and who holds their hand in the parking lot are all examples of age-appropriate choices.

When it's about time for the kids to come in from playing in the yard for dinner, instead of bellowing, "Time for dinner, you need to come in right now!" try a slightly different approach next time.

"Hey guys, it's about time for dinner. Do you want to come in now or play for a few more minutes?" And of course, the answer will always be, "We want to play longer."

"Do you want to play for three minutes or five?"

"Three," they say loudly and with much power. "Okay, I'll let you know when the time is up and then it will be time for dinner."

Three minutes later, you call out through the back door

"Time's up; time for dinner," and nine times out of ten they gladly come running in. Because *they* decided when it was time to come in for dinner. And when they are given opportunities to call the shots, they feel a sense of control over their lives and they cooperate. It's like magic.

So look around their entire day and find places where you can ask what *they* want and turn things over to them. "Do you want to sit on this side of the backseat or that side? Do you want me to buckle you in or can you do it? Do you want to pour your milk or let me do it?" The more they can dress themselves, pour their own cereal, open their own car door, and unlock the front door with the keys, the more they relax, because they are more in charge of their lives. They feel more powerful and competent. Involving them in discussions about how to handle common everyday issues like mornings, bedtime, mealtimes, etc., creates much greater cooperation as well (see Agreements and Accountability on pg. 61). Kids of all ages (including adults) love to have say-so in their home life, their classroom, their work environment. So give it freely.

• *Ask Their Opinion:* This tells kids you value their ideas and, therefore, you value them. "Do you think I need to wear a sweatshirt today? Should we have dinner on the porch tonight?" Engage their opinions as often as you can.

• *Let Them Teach You Things:* Kids love to teach their parents how to sing a song, do a new dance step, play a game from school, diagram a new basketball play, whatever. Even play dumb if you have to sometimes, because you know that when they are the teacher and you are the earnest pupil, this gives them a tremendous sense of empowerment.

• *Don't Do Things for Them That They Could or Should Be Doing for Themselves:* Such a situation makes a child feel impotent and it keeps them dependent. It may seem a lot easier and quicker in the short run to dress your five year old in the morning, but in the long run you've done her and yourself a disservice. It also creates a potential unnecessary power struggle every morning. All the little tasks that make up their day are potential important confidence builders, i.e., dress and feed themselves, brush their own teeth, shampoo their hair, pour the cereal, buckle their seat belt, clean up their eating place at the table, put their toys away. So allow them to do it themselves even if it causes them some frustration. Working through frustrations until they finally accomplish the task allows them to say with gusto, "I did it myself!" Now *that* is empowering!

• *Allow Your Kids to Say NO:* Allow them to set boundaries in your home, including with you! I remember one day seeing my son John, then about five, eating a bag of fruit candies. I asked him if I could have one, and he looked up at me and declared, "No!" On the outside, I said okay and walked away. But I must confess that on the inside I was not a happy camper. Thoughts started racing through my head; thoughts like, "you ungrateful little snot! How dare you say no to your father! Who do you think bought that candy?" Luckily I didn't express all of that old, authoritative garbage. And lo and behold, a minute later John walked up to me with a fruit dinosaur in his hands, and asked me if I wanted a piece of candy! You see, he didn't mind giving me one after all. The "no" was a test to see if he could set a boundary with me and if I would respect it.

For those of you reading this and freaking out and wondering what this sort of "liberal, permissive parenting" will teach the kids as far as sharing, I can reassure you that there are hundreds, nay thousands, of opportunities for kids to learn to share. And I think it's also important that kids feel comfortable setting boundaries, and taking care of themselves. Being able to practice this in the safety of their home with siblings and parents prepares them for setting boundaries on the playground in grade school and the backseat of their car in high school.

And I want to be perfectly clear that if you have a prior agreement with your child about something, then that is not an appropriate time for them to say no. If, for example, you agreed at a family meeting that the kids would put away their toys before they turned on the television in the evening, then it is not a choice for them to say no to toy pickup. "I know you want to watch your movie, but we have an agreement about picking up toys first. Let me know when you have that done and then I'll turn on the television." So there is no further discussion, just follow through on your agreement.

The times to allow kids to say no are situations that crop up spontaneously where the stakes are low and the issues not very important (like John's candy). For kids to grow up emotionally healthy, they need to be giving and empathetic, and they also need to feel comfortable setting boundaries in order to take good care of themselves.

• *Allow Kids to Hold You Accountable:* A great way for kids to feel powerful and respected is to be able to hold *you* to agreements you made with them.

"Mommy, remember you said no more yelling in our house." Teach them how to do this in a loving, respectful way so they can practice standing up for themselves, have a strong voice that gets results, and learn to hold people they love responsible for their agreements. Great preparation for marriage, wouldn't you agree?

• *Outlets for Aggression:* Be sure to supply kids with plenty of regular, healthy outlets for their aggression. Wrestling, dancing, giggling, and playing tag or soccer, are examples of fun ways to blow off steam and channel aggressive feelings. Preschoolers love to play dress-up, pretending to be a scolding mother, a gentle or mean teacher, a ferocious lion or monster, a meek lamb. They are trying out all parts of themselves and checking out the reactions they create with their drama, i.e., approval or displeasure. Using their creative imaginations through make-believe play is a healthy way to navigate through the turbulent waves of their aggression.

• *Who's Afraid of the Big Bad Wolf?:* Mastering their fears is another important task for 4- and 5-year-olds, and parents can play a big part by supporting them through this issue. Fears of the dark, monsters, dogs, bees, sirens, separations from parents, you name it and I'll find you a preschooler to match the fear. Developmentally, kids need to learn to face their fears, push through them, and master them by themselves with their parents on the periphery offering encouragement and support. However, parents should not be taking care of these fears for them. You want your four year old to walk into your bedroom one morning with a huge grin on their face and proudly exclaim, "I made it all night in my own room!" Mastering these fears gives confidence that they can be more independent and take care of themselves.

It's interesting and important to note that fears and aggressive feelings surface at the same time, as though to balance each other. Many kids use their aggressive feelings and play to overcome their fears. What better way to overcome fears of monsters than to become one? Becoming a growling mean tiger is one way to compensate for feeling fearful. That way they don't have to be afraid of the big bad wolf any longer.

SUMMARY

I often ask parents who are struggling with power-hungry preschoolers, "When does your child seem most happy and relaxed and when does everything at home seem to be most in sync? Besides when your 3-year-old is napping!"

And parents always have the same answer. It's when their child is being helpful or valuable; it's when they've listened enough to create a true win-win situation with their child; it's times when they've turned things over to their child causing them to feel more powerful and independent. Think about your own kids and I bet you'll come up with the same answers yourself. This is why the previous discussion about giving kids power is such an important piece to put into practice in your home. It truly is incredibly effective preventative medicine.

This is such an important age and stage for kids. By the time kids are ready for kindergarten at ages five to six years, they've integrated a lot of experiences and reactions into a picture of who they are and how they fit in, how much power and say-so they have in this world, how they can make things happen to get their needs met, what their limits and boundaries are and what is appropriate and what is not, how to channel their impulses and aggressive feelings into healthier, useful means, and how capable and competent they are. And remember that I'll take these general principles about power and control and say-so and agreements and apply them in later chapters to specific, common problem areas for many parents, i.e., mornings, after work, and evenings. But first let's discuss the growing-up stage for five- to seven-year-olds.

5

....

"I'm Running Away to Emerald City!" (Ages 5-7 Years)

This Emotional Growing-Up stage is often overlooked and misunderstood. If parents have done a reasonably effective job of redirecting the power struggles of their 2–3 year olds, there often is a period of relative calm when kids are 4–5 years old. They are invested less and less in engaging adults inappropriately because there are more important and fascinating learning experiences to attend to. Things like learning the alphabet, books, coloring, building elaborate Lego projects, friendships.

But then, all of a sudden, out of the blue, they throw a curveball at us. Parents see the return of fits, moodiness, crabbiness, impatience. They bark at parents a lot. Let me give you an example from my counseling practice.

*   *   *

"Mom, I'm riding my bike to Lori's," barked six-year-old Audrey to her mom as she headed out the door.

"Wait a minute Audrey. That's too far for you to go without Dad or me with you. I can take you in twenty minutes," yelled Mom from the other room.

"Why can't I go by myself?" screamed Audrey. "All my friends can ride their bikes to *my* house! It's not fair! You never let me do anything! I hate you, and I hate this stupid family! I'm running away!" Whew, what a mouthful. And Audrey would then proceed to throw things around and grunt and complain; all the while her mother is in the kitchen wondering *what happened* and *what did I do wrong now* and *I thought we were through the temper tantrum stage a year ago.*

This scenario sounds awful teen-like doesn't it? It does so, because, like teenagers, kids at 5–7 years of age are going through an important emotional growing up. And any time any one of us goes through such a transition, i.e., at 18 months, 5–7 years, teens, mid-life crisis, we get out-of-sorts. There is a kind of internal emotional upheaval. So let's dissect this stage as we did the previous two.

LESSONS A CHILD LEARNS

• *Home-body to World-body:* Most of a child's important learning about relationships, loveability, trust, closeness, sharing, and empathy in the first five years occurs in the home, with their parents and siblings as teachers and models. The important relationship foundations put down in order to be available for future learning in school and life are built primarily through interactions with family. Even if kids spend a lot of time at day care, they know who butters their bread and who will stick with them through thick and thin. That's why I call preschoolers "home-bodies." All the sibling fights and, for single kids, the triangles they set up between themselves and their parents, are the canvas on which these important relationship lessons are learned and later drawn from.

If you fast-forward a couple years and check out the life of a 7- or 8-year-old, there has been a major shift in where their important life and relationship lessons occur. Now most of the learning is out in the world, at school, on the soccer field, in the neighborhood, at friends' houses. Kids become close to school teachers, piano teachers, coaches, friends' parents. They need to take all the lessons they learned about relationships and getting along in the first five years and apply them now to friends (usually same-sex friends) and other important adults involved with them. They come home from school, drop their book bags on the table, grab a handful of cookies, and they are out the door to "go play at Lori's house." And, all of this is natural and on target.

• *Expressing Their Feelings in Healthy Ways:* Learning to express feelings, and to ask specifically for what they want in ways that are effective are very important tasks for children at this age. Whining, screaming, barking, and complaining need to be replaced by telling people how they feel and what they want.

• *Time to Stretch:* Most parents of kids this age will report that sometimes they will see their child act very mature, or say something wise and deep and they will think WOW, my kid has really grown up. And then in the next moment they see their child regress and act like a three year old. Thumbsucking, carrying around blankets, baby talking, and whining to get their parents to do things for them are just a few examples of what the regressions might look like.

Kids between ages 5 and 7 seem to be caught between two worlds. I want to grow up and I don't. I want more freedom and responsibility and a longer leash *and* I want to be taken care of and more dependent. And out of this ambivalence about growing up comes the disruption. This is why kids in this transition seem out of sorts and crabby. They do and they don't. Sounds like two year olds and teenagers doesn't it?

FEELINGS WITHIN THE CHILD

• *Ambivalence:* Often the most common feeling at this stage is I want to grow up and be out in the world *and* I want to be home being coddled and taken care of like when I was younger. Having an older sibling on hand often presses the child forward to wanting to grow up. And conversely, having younger siblings at home being taken care of by Mom and Dad may pull your six year old backward, not wanting to go to school or a friend's party because they'll miss out on whatever's going on with their younger siblings on the homefront.

Precocious 4½-year-old Mary Jane was involved in a major power struggle with her mom over toilet training. And as is always the case when it comes to a battle over the bathroom, Mary Jane was winning. One day during a battle over getting dressed, out of nowhere Mary Jane blurted out, "Mommy, if I go poop on the toilet and dress myself, will you still take care of me?" She was early for getting into this stage, but right on target with her question, which I think is at the heart of this ambivalence in 5–6 year olds.

I remember one day playing catch in the backyard with my then six-year-old son, T.J. We'd only been throwing for a few moments when two doors down some kids started playing basketball. T.J. looked kind of longingly toward the kids, then back at me as we played catch. I could sense his ambivalence: do I want to stay home and play catch with Dad, or go play with my friends? So I said to him, "T.J., if you want to play with your friends, that's okay with me." He said, "No, I want to play catch with you." So we threw the ball back and forth a few more times, and then he looked over to me and said a little sheepishly, "I want to play basketball now." He threw down his glove and excitedly raced over to the neighbor's yard. To me, that was a perfect example of his internal struggle about transitioning from a "home-body" to a "world-body."

- *"My Stomach Hurts!"*: During this stage, a lot of children, especially girls, tend to have a lot of aches—stomach aches, headaches, leg aches, etc. These aches are really a result of "internalized growing pains." The ambivalence described above causes kids to feel confused, out-of-sorts, moody, upset, angry. The kids who tend to internalize their feelings hold on to these emotions, which then tend to settle in some part of the body. All of us, adults and kids, have a place in our bodies where we tend to hold our stress. It might be our head (headaches, migraines), our stomach (aches, butterflies, irritable bowel), our back (low back pain), or our muscles (tight jaw or neck or back muscles). So it makes sense that the stresses from this important stage might surface as body aches.

And they actually do experience these aches, just like you really do have a migraine. The aren't faking it. So dismissing their somatic complaints will actually create more emotions and more aches.

- *"I'm Running Away!"*: Angry outbursts are common during this stage. Little fits, yelling at parents, and stomping around are examples of how their upset is expressed. Here are some common verbal shots:

"I hate you!"

"You don't understand!"

"That's not fair!"

"I wish I was adopted!"

"I'm running away!"

The typical kid in the old stories who was running away was about six, with a stick over his shoulder and his belongings all wrapped up. When he gets to the street corner, he turns back because he's not supposed to cross the street alone. Or he lasts out in the world about three hours until the snacks run out.

Kids who are more intense, outgoing, and who wear their emotions on their sleeves (as opposed to the more quiet internalizers) will express the feelings brought on by this stage. They bark a lot, complain, yell, and then they feel a lot better. They get the feelings out, so these types of kids don't experience the aches like some of their friends.

FEELINGS ELICITED IN PARENTS

• *Confusion Leading to Frustration and Anger:* Because most parents don't understand why their kids are so out-of-sorts, they feel confused about why their kids are suddenly flipping out again. They get frustrated because nothing seems to curb the crabbiness for very long. And then many parents get angry because they are sick of the constant emotional drama.

• *Hurt:* Many parents feel hurt when their kids say mean and angry things to them. And kids are good at knowing their parents' soft spots. So a single mom might hear, "I hate you and I hate living here. I'd much rather live with Dad!" Ouch! Working parents often hear, "You're never home anyway. Why should you care?" Or, "You never come to my school parties like the other moms."

As described above, kids usually walk away feeling better after venting some feelings, acting like nothing happened. Parents who take the venting on or take it to heart are often left emotionally drained and a wreck.

• *Ambivalence:* If this is your youngest child, the "baby," it might be a little tough to let them go and grow up on you. Some parents hold on to that last child a little tighter, doing things for them and "babying them."

• *Worry:* Some parents misinterpret the fits and moodiness as a sign of poor self-esteem. So they become more anxious and worried about whether or not their kid is okay, whether they are depressed or unhappy.

PARENTS' REACTIONS

• *Punitive/Controlling:* When parents allow themselves to get frustrated and angry, oftentimes their next response is to become punitive. They shout back and get more restrictive. "You are grounded!" becomes part of the parent's arsenal. They hope that taking things away will cause their kids to settle down. This never works for long.

Because they feel their kids are out of control and "spoiled," parents often become more controlling. And since this is a time when kids need a little more freedom and rope, this really backfires. And it can create a lot of unnecessary arguments and power struggles that you thought you were done with.

• *"Well Then Go Live with Your Father!":* Many times when parents feel hurt by their kids, they react by hurting back. "Well I don't love you much today either." Yelling, spanking, disrespect, and punishments are reactions to our hurt feelings. This is how cycles of hurt and revenge get established.

• *Invalidation:* Some parents dismiss or brush off their child's feelings at this stage. "You don't have it so bad" or "You're always faking a stomachache right before school" are examples of how parents can invalidate feelings. And it's because they don't understand what's *really* going on for their child.

• *Overreactions to Somatic Complaints:* Excessive worry can cause some parents to pursue exhaustive medical work-ups and treatments for the stomachaches and headaches.

It is rare that anything shows up on the tests, so the aches are written off as Irritable Bowel Syndrome or early migraines. And unfortunately many kids are placed on one or more medications, many times unnecessarily. Parents aren't addressing the *real* issue which is to support their child through this important growing-up stage. And in my experience, overemphasis on the medications and physical symptoms causes more aches and more side effects, not fewer. And kids (and their parents) miss out on a chance to learn healthy ways to handle their powerful emotions.

Many times the child's somatic complaints become the central focus of the entire family, involving grandparents and aunts and uncles. When Grandma calls, the first thing out of her mouth is: "How is Julie's stomach this morning?" When we focus a lot of energy on anything, positive or negative, we tend to create more of it.

GHOSTS IN THE NURSERY

• *Parental Separation Issues:* There are many issues that can cause parents to be overprotective and have a difficult time letting their 6-year-olds grow up. Single parents often feel guilty about having put their child through a divorce or about not having the other parent around. They often work one or more jobs to make ends meet, thus causing them to spend a lot of time away from their kids. I see a lot of single parents who sleep with their young children because they miss being with them all day and they like having a warm body next to them at nighttime. I'm not saying that this is wrong, but in some cases it may cause parents to treat the child as if they are younger than they are and thereby keep them more dependent.

Parents who are "needy," who are insecure and unhappy, also have a tough time when their kids go through stages when they become more autonomous and need their space. Needy parents experience this as rejection, and they may treat their kids in ways that cause them to feel guilty about growing up and becoming more independent. They don't freely and encouragingly send their kids out in the world. Becoming a world-body becomes tainted with feelings of guilt and insecurity, so some kids become more anxious and stay dependent.

Six-year-old Mike came into my office with his doting parents because they were concerned about his anger and aggression toward them. I noticed how Mike crossed his parents' boundaries in small ways while his parents sheepishly grinned as if to say, "What can you do?" He got into Mom's purse even though she warned him against it three times. He curled up on his mom's lap a couple times and she stroked him as you would an infant or toddler. Then Mike's mom told me a long story about how she had tried to get pregnant for six years; how horrible an ordeal all the tests and failures were for them. When she finally got pregnant it was proclaimed "a miracle." After delivery, Mom was told she could never have more kids. So Mike grew up in a home where he was *everything* to his parents.

Mike's dad sarcastically told me to ask his wife why she was wearing a beeper. She replied tearfully that she wanted to be sure to be available for him in case anything happened. "He means everything to me. So if anything ever happened to him and he died, I'd die too." This was the ghost that made it hard for Mike's mom to let go.

• *"By God, I'll Be There for My Kids!"*: Parents who felt abandoned or rejected growing up often make a deep commitment to themselves that someday when they become a parent, they will be there for their kids, because they don't want their kids to ever have to experience the intense pain and hurt they grew up with. This can feel like smothering to a six year old ready to burst out into the world. Parents with this ghost have a hard time not being overly involved in every aspect of their child's life. And when some expressive kids feel smothered, they react with a lot of anger. This causes their parents to feel hurt and resentful and to withdraw from their kids. Which is what their child wanted in the first place—room to spread their wings. It's unfortunate that they have to create such chaos and mischief in order to achieve the space they need to grow.

• *Abuse/Molestation/Trauma:* Any parent who lived through one of these experiences brings some intense feelings into parenting: fear, terror, anger, powerlessness. They don't want their child to experience what they did, so they often become overprotective.

Six-year-old Jenny was enraged at her mom because she wasn't being allowed to ride her bike to her best friend Julie's house a block away. They went through major arguments and power struggles almost daily. When I asked Mom about her childhood, she recalled tearfully how she had been molested by a neighborhood teenage boy when she was about seven years old. And when she told her parents, no one believed her. So when her daughter Jenny got close to that age, her old feelings of terror resurfaced, making it hard for her to let Jenny too far out of her sight because she was afraid something might happen to her.

HEALTHY, EFFECTIVE PARENTING FOR THE EMOTIONAL GROWING-UP STAGE

• *Let GO!:* Parents need to do whatever it takes for them to become aware of their ghosts and handle them so that they can provide the space and "rope" that kids need to grow up.

*　　*　　*

When our son, John, was ten years old, he started asking for permission to ride his bike with his friend to a pizza place about a mile away. At first we were reluctant. But we recognized his need to have more freedom and responsibility, and that our primary concern was the busy street he'd be riding on. So we took him on several bike rides to this place, allowing him to show us he knew how to stop at each intersection, look both ways, and take good care of himself. At that point, we allowed him to go with his friend.

Kids need more and more opportunities to be on their own and to make choices and age-appropriate decisions for themselves. When most of us were growing up, we had the run of the neighborhood and nearby woods to explore with our buddies without adult supervision. We had lots of chances to be on our own out in the world. I think many kids are missing out on that today because parental fears escalate as we hear horror stories of bad things happening to kids every day. So look for opportunities that allow kids to spread their wings.

It can be especially tough for working parents to provide these opportunities. They may not have had the time to get to know the kids in the neighborhood and their parents, or the kids in their child's class or on the soccer team. I have noticed that in neighborhoods with a lot of families where both parents work, that parents are seldom outside playing with kids. Working parents arrive home tired, and they have just enough energy left to handle routines like dinner, house cleaning, and yard maintenance. But they have no reserves left for basketball games or to be the all-time quarterback for football games.

But the bottom line is that you need to create this time. I see tons of perfectly manicured lawns that took away play time with kids. You may have to let go of having to have the perfect yard, a pristine clean house, and gourmet meals and instead focus on more time to connect with the neighborhood. Get out there and play goalie for the roller hockey game, ride bikes around the block and be sure to stop and chat with your child's friends' parents. Get to know them so that you feel safe to let your kids spend time away from home. Have your kids show you their bike routes, shortcuts, and favorite hangouts. Have a party for the soccer team after a weekend game so that you become closer to those parents too.

If you're thinking that this all sounds great, but . . . I don't have the time, then I'm going to strongly encourage you to reorganize your life a bit so that your priorities shift some. Your young clingy children will be busy teens before you know it. They really do grow up fast. They need space and freedom to explore and grow up, so make it a priority that you create a safety net around them. A safety net of caring neighbors, coaches, and families that allows you to trust that your kids are okay and safe when you're not with them. A safety net that allows you to let go.

• *Forward Ho!:* Going along with the point above, look for ways to help kids stretch forward versus plugging into their regressions. Investing too much energy into the baby-talking or fits or body-aches causes more of those. Investing energy into creating stretching experiences nudges kids forward, where they are headed developmentally. Give them more responsibility, more places to be helpful and valuable. Allow them some "perks" for being older versus lumping them too much with their younger sibling. Let them stay up a little later, have more freedoms, watch different movies. Most kids at this stage love being treated this way. It's honoring and empowering. They sense that their parents understand them and their needs. And it's great preparation for parenting in the teen years.

• *Detach!:* Don't take on your child's emotions, i.e., don't take them personally. The "I hate you's!" don't mean that they are rejecting you or will hate you forever or that you've lost your child. Don't allow yourself to get frustrated, angry, or "plugged in" to their mischief or emotions. Remember that these important transitions create more than enough emotions within kids. Adding any of ours to the mix makes it overwhelming for everyone. Kids whose feelings are going up and down need calm, centered people around them for balance and security. So do whatever you need to do to stay present and calm and loving and patient and understanding.

• *"So What I Hear You Saying Is . . .":* Listen mostly to the feelings behind the words and the mischief, as opposed to reacting to the words. Learn how to mirror their feelings back to them; "Sounds like you feel frustrated with us because we won't let you ride your bike to your friend's house."

Let them know you hear them, that their feelings are valid, and that you understand where they are coming from (even if you don't agree). Mirroring and validating are great tools to dissipate the intense emotions and energy. Kids need a safe place to let their hair down and vent and get real. I'd rather have them do this at home where you can help them deal with these feelings in healthy ways.

• *Ask and You Shall Receive:* Teach kids appropriate ways to ask for what they want instead of whining and complaining. Whenever kids tell me "it's not fair," I first listen to what they are saying. I let them know I hear them, then I ask them to switch it by telling me what they want. They'll get a lot more in life if they've learned how to ask for what they want in ways that are effective.

• *Redirect the Regressions!:* Instead of getting all bent out of shape by their regressions, just redirect them in a kind but firm manner: "It's hard for me to understand you when you're whining. Use your regular voice please."

And if they don't switch it, ACT immediately. "As soon

as you can use your regular voice to tell me what you want, come see me." And with that, detach from the impending power struggle and argument. Walk away so you don't get sucked into their drama and wait for them to come to you when they are calmer.

• *Drama 101:* It's okay and normal for kids at this age to be dramatic. Don't ridicule it or be sarcastic about it, because that hurts their feelings. Accept that it's a normal part of going through an important growing-up period.

• *Dates:* Since in some ways I'm asking you to detach from their drama and power struggles, it's important that you replace that with special one-on-one time. So "attach" in fun, appropriate ways as you "detach" from getting plugged into the games. The same will hold true for the teen years. Give them more space and freedom and rope, and be sure to connect with them in special ways and be there for them when they return from their ventures out in the world. It gives kids a much-needed sense of security that they have loving, supportive parents backing them up as they navigate life's ups and downs.

Now that we've covered these three important stages, it's time to turn to learning healthy ways to redirect the power struggles most families face most days. Let's start with mornings.

Part 2

....

Redirection Time

....

6

················

"Morning Has Broken" Taming Those Morning Monsters

Ringggg!!! Whack! The lovely sounds of your alarm clock going off awakening you to another day. And this day brings round 1,463 in the struggle for morning time supremacy with your preschooler. If you lost the bedtime battle last night, you need only roll over to the other side of your bed to face your child and the wake-up scene. If you were lucky last night, you are now required to plod into your child's room to wake her up. What waking up typically requires is three to four trips into her room with escalating pitch and volume in your voice, several total body uncoverings, and finally, leading them into the bathroom. At this point the whining usually starts.

"I don't want to go to school today! I want to stay home. You never stay home with me anymore. How come Joey gets to stay home with his mom?" At this point the child throws out as many hooks as possible, hoping to catch one of your sensitive heartstrings. Hoping to start reeling you into "The Game." The debate begins.

"Look, I told you last night I have to go to work today."

"I thought you said tomorrow," she whines.

"You know you have fun once you get to school," you plead, feeling somewhat guilty.

"I don't want to go!" she declares more emphatically.

"I'm not going to argue with you today." (P.S. You already are!) "Go into your room right now and get dressed!" Anger and frustration now creep into your voice.

At this point kids often start screaming or they may run to their room muttering four-year-old profanity equivalents like: "You're so stupid. I hate you!" Some kids will throw themselves on the floor and dig their heels in. The parent retreats into their own bedroom to attempt to get showered and dressed. Halfway through the shower many parents hear whining outside the shower door, which ruins what should have been a relaxing few moments. Parents banter back and forth between scrubs and drying off, with the only result being a more frustrated parent and a still-not-dressed, whiny child. During the next twenty minutes the parents get dressed piecemeal in between threats and arguments and bribes with their child.

"If you get dressed right now I'll let you watch cartoons during breakfast," Mom bribes.

"Can I sit at the counter?" she asks, with an I'm-starting-to-win grin on her face.

"Okay, but only if you get dressed by yourself and let me have time to myself to get ready."

"Okay, but can you just help me get this shirt on?"

"All right, but you have to do the rest yourself." Sure. Ten minutes, four threats, two yells, and twenty systolic blood pressure points later, you've somehow managed to completely dress your child and feel resentful as all-get-out. The resentment carries over into extra barking and control in your voice during the fight about what to eat for breakfast. This morning you were lucky. You only had to make two different breakfasts before your child started eating. But, of course, now you have exactly fifteen minutes to get dressed, fed, and otherwise prepared for *your* day! The pressure mounts as the minutes tick away. You arrive back in the kitchen, with no time to spare, to find your child's clothes have taken on the color and texture of her breakfast and that she has also taken her shoes off. You quickly and roughly put her shoes back on, wipe off her clothes as best you can and deny the stains left over with the thought that no one will probably see it and no one will judge you as a bad parent because of it.

You are already late before you even attempt the next part of the morning—leaving the house. This request often provokes screaming for more television, major struggles around jamming shoes back on, yelling while you pull and drag her all the way out to the car. Somehow, using your four years of high school wrestling experience, you manage to stuff your daughter into the car seat. You are late, stressed and frustrated. During the ride to preschool, even turning the radio volume to full blast fails to drone out the high level screaming from the backseat. On arrival at the daycare center, you drag your screaming child with the stained clothes down the hall to her classroom, with that desperately-trying-to-look-cool-and-in-control fake smile on your face that all parents can relate to. The fantasy departure scene of hugs and kisses and sweet words is long forgotten. You give the teacher a weak smile as she pulls the clinging child off your legs. You float back to your car and slump behind the wheel feeling inadequate, exhausted, guilty, and deflated. And, you are, as usual, late!

Whew! Kind of depressing, isn't it? Well, you've come to the right place in the book because it's time to talk about redirecting these morning struggles.

The first bit of advice is to remember the developmental reasons why kids engage us in these struggles as we discussed in chapters three, four, and five. Use this understanding to help *you* stay disciplined and detached. You have got to discipline yourself and refuse to fight. Refuse to argue. Refuse to yell and threaten. Refuse to bribe or give in. Refuse to "plug in" by getting flustered and angry. And you must learn to teach kids that you are not willing to play this game through your *actions*, not through lip-service lectures. Your attitude needs to be kind and loving (no yelling, spanking, threatening) yet firm (clear, detached, following through with agreements). When children sense this clear, firm intention in their parents, cooperation usually follows.

Having the right attitude is of utmost importance. But, it's not enough. You also must learn to implement a new model at home to create cooperation. Here are some important steps crucial to this model.

- Make prior agreements with kids in a democratic manner.

- Don't come across with an accusatory tone or else kids "leave their bodies" immediately (i.e., "I'm sick and tired of you making me late for work!").

- Give kids lots of say-so in how the agreements will look instead of making it seem like the king and queen (Dad and Mom) are handing down edicts periodically.

- Really listen to their ideas. Mirror back to them what you hear them saying to be sure you both are clear about how they want things to work.

- Add your two cents worth. It is best to hear their thoughts first, but it is very important that you set appropriate boundaries that take care of your needs also.

- Create a win-win solution that uses as many of your child's ideas as possible and what works for both of you.

- Be sure before leaving the negotiation table that everyone is clear about the agreement. This requires extra time and patience up front but pays huge dividends down the road as I will explain later. Be sure your child is clear about what you are willing to do and what you are not willing to do.

- Acknowledge your child for her efforts in creating the win-win solution.

- End with the agreement that you'll try out the new plan for a few weeks and see how it goes.

- This model is best accomplished in the setting of a family meeting.

Let's use the previous morning-mayhem example to walk through what the language might look like with your child using this new model.

First off, don't try to have this discussion five minutes before you are supposed to leave. Instead, find a quiet time when there is no conflict going on and when your concern is not an issue in that moment. It might be during a family meeting, or maybe before bedtime when you're sitting on their bed rubbing their back and sharing the events of your day.

"Sally, I've got a problem I need help with. Do you have some time to talk now?" Asking permission like this is especially important as kids get older, and it's essential when they hit their teen years. At this point, if they agree to talk, it is crucial that you start out by owning your part in the problem.

"I know that I've been nagging at you in the mornings about getting dressed and stuff. And most of the time I end up yelling at you and I don't like how I feel after I drop you off at school. And I imagine you don't like how it feels either. Does that sound about right?"

"Yeah, I don't like it when you yell at me."

"I didn't think you did. Well, I need some help to make the mornings more fun, and I'm also not willing to be late for work anymore. So how do you think we can handle mornings better?" At this point some parents have to take out the duct tape and seal their mouths shut! It's so easy to start yapping and not listen to their ideas. In my experience, once kids get to be anywhere from 2½ to 3½ years of age, depending primarily on their language abilities, you can start this type of process. And you may be surprised by what you hear. Surprised at how well they express their ideas. Surprised because their ideas are usually pretty simi-

At a family meeting in the Jordan house several years ago, our family came up with a plan whereby everyone's order of the morning would be as follows:

1. Wake up
2. Bathroom duties, including teeth
3. Get yourself dressed
4. Make your bed
5. Come downstairs for breakfast
6. Out the door for school

Our kids decided on their own that they didn't want any TV watching before school. They said it especially wasn't fair that their then-preschool-age brother, John, could watch cartoons while they couldn't because they were getting ready for school. This agreement has worked for our family for many years now. Every household will have different schedules and personalities and values. There is no correct morning agreement. The important part is that everyone has a say-so, everyone is heard, everyone's ideas are validated, as much of the plan as possible comes from the kids, and your boundaries are respected, i.e., you're not late for work.

lar to our ideas and not off the wall and selfish like we often expect. Surprised at how excited kids are about this process.

"So let me make sure I've heard this agreement right. What I heard us say is that we'll wake you up in the morning, and you'll brush your teeth and get dressed and make your beds before you come down for breakfast. If you come

to the table without having done the above then we'll remind you about our agreement and you won't be able to
eat until that part is done. We'll remind you once when
there is about ten minutes to go before we have to leave
so that you're on time for school and I'm on time for work.
If you're not ready when it's time to go, I'll put your clothes
and shoes in your bag and take you out to the car and you
can finish getting dressed at school. I won't nag or yell or
argue with you, and I'm not willing to leave late. Is that
what you heard too?"

"Yeah, Dad, but you forgot about no TV."

"Right, and no TV before school. Let's try it out for a
few weeks and see how it goes. Thanks for your help and
cooperation."

At this point, you can breathe a sigh of relief, because
you never have to argue or debate about this issue again.
All you have to do is follow through with this clear
agreement. And follow through without any frustration,
anger, arguing, or reminding. If the next day your child
comes to the breakfast table in her pj's then kindly but
firmly ask her to go get dressed before breakfast. If she
starts to whine or argue, say to her, "I'm not willing to
argue, we have an agreement." Then zip up your lips and,
if necessary, walk away. Kids are good at reeling us in, so
do whatever it takes to stay detached. Take a shower, leave
the room, leave them with their tantrum.

Those first few days some kids will literally and sometimes figuratively throw the book at you. Their whining and screaming may escalate to unheard-of levels in their quest to get you involved in the old tug-of-war games or to get you to give in. Some kids just can't believe you are finally holding firm. You can almost hear their brains saying, "Well, yesterday all it took was thirty decibels for fifteen minutes to get my way. Maybe if I raise it to fifty decibels for twenty minutes that will do the trick." I tell parents that it is vital to stay out of it and to follow through and leave on time. If it means taking a half dressed, hungry kid to preschool to the judgmental stares of the whole world, so be it. Be sure you are calm and *don't* fire any shots at the kids, i.e., "I hope this makes you happy. I told you I wasn't putting up with your junk anymore!" Call the preschool ahead of time and explain what you are up to. I've never had a school not cooperate happily. And, in my experience with thousands of parents, it rarely takes more than one or two such mornings, *if* you stay detached and *if* you follow through.

- *Lessons Kids Learn from This Model:*
  - I have a lot of say-so in the agreements around here, and it feels good to be able to express my thoughts and feelings and to be heard.

  - It feels empowering to have my ideas used in the solutions and to have as much say-so as my older sibling.

- My parents follow through on our agreements, therefore, my parents mean what they say.

- I can't induce my parents to play tug-of-war with me no matter how high I intensify my mischief. Therefore, I'll give up this method of trying to get what I want.

- I get more of what I want and it feels better when there is cooperation and when I ask for things in a respectful, effective way.

- *Lessons Parents Learn from This Model:*
  - I can gain more cooperation with a lot less effort if I learn to detach.

  - By disciplining myself to stay detached, I avoid feeling all of the frustration, anger, guilt, and helplessness I used to feel.

  - By being more clear and firm with my boundaries, my kids become more relaxed, cooperative, empowered, and happy.

  - By taking the time up front to listen to my kids and create real win-win solutions, I avoid wasting time engaged in power struggles down the road.

And together, parents and their children will have more time for eating breakfast together, conversation, and singing songs in the car. The separations at preschool will be more secure and loving. Parents will feel more relaxed and confident about working and leaving their children in day care. Working parents will arrive at work on time and be ready to get to work. The family will eliminate that tense, "rushed," distant feeling in the mornings.

Now, before we move on to redirecting afternoon struggles, I can hear a bunch of parents out there grumbling, "What about my 18-month-old who doesn't talk yet and who's neck-deep in the 'terrible two's'?" So let's address how to redirect these preverbal kids.

Jackie brought her 18-month-old daughter, Gail, in to see me because of intense battles in the mornings over getting her dressed. Up until about fifteen months, Gail had been "such an easy, good baby." But it seemed like one day a switch was turned on and suddenly Gail was "acting like a monster. It was like Jekyl and Hyde," Jackie told me. "I don't know what we're doing wrong."

I reassured Jackie that Gail was normal and that her character change was a normal symptom of her autonomy stage. Those words seemed to relax Jackie immensely. "What can I do about getting her dressed in the mornings?"

Jackie had told me that Gail seemed to do better when she kept her schedule pretty constant. So I encouraged her to decide on a morning routine that worked best for her and that would allow her to get to work on time. Then she was to follow through on that schedule no matter what.

"What should I do when she refuses to let me dress her?" asked Jackie. I asked her to describe what exactly happened during these scenes. Jackie said Gail would let her change her diaper without much of a fuss, but as soon as she started trying to put on her dress or skirt, Gail would start flailing at her, occasionally landing a blow to Mom.

"At that point, I've gotten angry at her and then kind of roughly hold her down and forced the clothes on her. It's not a very pretty sight, believe me," explained Jackie. I suggested that Jackie give Gail some choices about what to wear each day. "Do you want to wear your sundress or this outfit?" Sometimes just giving a toddler a simple choice like that prevents the struggles. If she picks the dress, and then starts to resist your putting it on, I would immediately disengage, being very careful and on-guard to prevent her from hitting you, and I'd say to her, "I'm not willing to be hit, and I'm not willing to fight you to get you dressed. As soon as you calm yourself and are ready to let me dress you, I'll come back. Once you are dressed we can go down to breakfast. Let me know when you are ready." With that said, I told Jackie to walk out of her room and stay calm.

I warned Jackie that this might very well lead to an explosion of anger from Gail, since toddlers don't like it when their parents won't fight and when parents walk away from them. And that it was okay if Gail lost it for awhile, and it was okay to let her blow off steam in her room like that.

I told Jackie to check back in on her every five to ten minutes. "Are you ready for me to dress you yet?" If the answer was an emphatic **"NO!!!"** then Jackie was to calmly tell her again that as soon as she was ready, she'd dress her and then take her down to breakfast. And again to walk out of her room. I advised Jackie to leave an extra 30 to 40 minutes for these "training sessions" for several days. So she would need to set the alarm for an earlier wake up and perhaps an earlier bedtime. And to be committed to seeing it through no matter how many mornings it took.

Once Gail was calmed down and ready to be dressed, Jackie could go back into her room and say, "Thanks for calming yourself. Which shirt do you want to wear today? This one or that one?" and very matter-of-factly go on with the morning's routine. No lecture or rehashing of the events is necessary. What Jackie is saying to Gail, in essence, is: "It's okay to lose it when you are 18 months old, and you can count on me not to join in. I'll allow you to cool down, then we'll go on with our day."

And it won't take Jackie more than a week or so to switch her and Gail's mornings around. Many working parents have told me that they don't have that kind of time to spend in the mornings training their kids. My response to that is that they already are spending that time training

106

their kids, but they are training them to argue, resist, whine, throw tantrums, and play tug-of-war. Why not get a healthy, long-term plan in place and follow it through. Because after a short time, you will be done with all the morning chaos and fights.

Whether you use a family meeting discussion with older kids or just a brief, simple explanation with actions that back it up with younger kids, they really do sense when we mean it. If you follow through with your boundaries consistently even with an 18-month-old, and especially if you do it without any emotion (anger, frustration, control) kids learn to respect the boundaries and cooperate.

So, get started in creating the smooth-running, peaceful, cooperative morning you've been dreaming of for your home. Next we will discuss how to redirect those after-work reunions that we all want to look forward to but oftentimes dread because of the mischief involved.

7

....

"Take This Job and . . ."
Getting a Handle on the
After Work/Day-care Chaos

It is 5:30 P.M. as Mary Jo pulls her van into the parking lot of her daughter Linda's preschool. Exhausted by her own tough day at work, she trudges into the center expecting the worst. And why wouldn't she, considering that each evening for the past three months she has been greeted by an out-of-control, crabby 3½-year-old.

"I'm here honey, time to go home and get some dinner," Mary Jo gamely greets Linda. Linda, glued to the center's TV screen, acts like she doesn't even hear her mom.

"Honey, it's time to go home," Mom says.

"I don't want to go home now! I want to see the movie!" exclaims Linda.

"Linda, we have this movie at home, so you can finish it there. Let's get your backpack."

"I want to stay," cries out Linda, digging her heels in more.

When Mary Jo goes over to try to guide Linda away from the television, all you-know-what breaks loose. Linda starts to scream and kick and flop around, which makes the late-shift day-care teacher quickly come over to try to restore order. "Come on Linda. We can watch this tomorrow," she says. Linda begrudgingly goes to get her backpack and coat. And at that point, the teacher turns to Mom and pierces her right in the heart.

"I don't know what got into her. She's been a perfect angel all day." Ouch!

So Mary Jo grabs Linda's hand and they walk out the door. Halfway to the car, Linda starts whining.

"I'm hungry. Can we go to McDonald's?"

"No honey, we've been there twice this week already. And I have something planned for dinner already."

Linda immediately melts to dead weight, requiring Mary Jo to pick her up and carry her to the car, where another fight breaks out about not wanting to sit in her car seat. Once that step is handled, Mary Jo is left with a steady stream of wailing from the backseat all the way home. When they pull into the driveway, Linda refuses to get out, whereby Mom throws up her arms in defeat, and with tears in her eyes, trudges into the house wondering if it's all worth it. Linda remains in her car seat for several more minutes, screaming for her mother to come help her out of the car. When she finally realizes Mom's not coming, she climbs out of the car and marches into the house with fire in her eyes, looking for the next round.

And so begins another family's evening of Quality Time. You can imagine or probably know from experience, that the evening progresses with a continuation of the previous hour's antics, with one power struggle blending into the next. Potential sites are the dinner table, the bath tub, and the bedroom. Throw in toilet training and you've got a real bonanza to look forward to each evening. So let's look at some ways for parents first to prevent the struggles and also how to handle them should they occur.

But first a few words about what's going on for young children after preschool or when their parents get home from work. During my year of Behavioral Pediatrics fellowship training with Dr. T. Berry Brazelton at the Child Development Center at Harvard, I got to spend a lot of time at a local preschool. One day a week the fellows got to sit in on a classroom from morning drop-off time to closing time. We observed the kids, played with them and learned a great deal through this process.

One of the things we all noticed was the phenomenon described above, where kids seemed to "fall apart" at the end of their day. It seemed as though they kept a lid on their extreme emotions, had fun, and played and laughed and cried, but it was as if they knew that this place wasn't home and therefore not safe enough to reveal and share *all* of their treasures. So they seemed to store up some of these feelings, saving them for the people they trusted the most, their parents. This accounted for why kids fell apart as soon as Mom or Dad stepped foot into the day-care center.

And if you think about it, these preschoolers are no different than gradeschoolers or teenagers or adults—all of whom don't feel safe enough to share all of their feelings and thoughts to friends or co-workers or bosses. So they all tend to feel safer at home to "let their hair down" and to vent or be crabby or silly at the end of their school day or work day.

I also see these end-of-the-day fits as a child's way of saying, "I miss you, and I feel a little disconnected from you. It was a tough day dealing with all of those 3 year olds, and I need some hugs and some loving." If you miss this piece, you'll miss out on the preventative medicine possibilities as well.

In previous chapters, we've gone over the influence of the child's current developmental stage on their behavior, as well as the role of the parent's reactions in either furthering or redirecting the mischief. Always keep these factors in mind, as they are critical for your understanding and awareness about what's going on.

Parents' Feelings: "What Have I Done Wrong Now?"

You can see how easily a parent's guilt buttons could be pushed by this behavior: Maybe I shouldn't be working outside the home. Maybe day care isn't such a good idea for my child. Maybe I should stay at home like my mom keeps saying. Maybe I'm not giving her enough quality time. Maybe we should have never had kids! I bet many of these thoughts have crossed your minds, especially at about 6:00 P.M. in the middle of all the chaos.

Remember the results of my survey in the introductory chapter? Most parents reported feeling tired, guilty, and drained. And most felt that their self-esteem suffered as a result of feeling inadequate as a parent because of these power struggles. It's hard not to question yourself and your career when you get the kind of reward Mary Jo got from the day-care teacher. Or when your parents or in-laws have been judging you negatively for working outside the home and putting your kids into day care. Or when you read the paper and see that 75 percent of day-care programs are judged by experts to be inadequately meeting children's needs. Or when you see your precious child flopping around on the floor wailing at you five evenings a week, acting as though they've been tortured all day.

Solutions

Fortunately, there are ways to smooth over those moments of transitions.

• *Work to Day-care Center:* Some parents have found it helpful to take care of their needs a bit before they pick up their kids. Maybe stop at the YMCA and work out for 45 minutes. Or take a walk at a local park. Or stop at a church and have some quiet time. Just take a little time to unwind and let go of your day. Because if you rush into a day-care center feeling crabby and late and drained, your kids will sense that immediately. And many kids will respond to their parent's feelings of distraction and weariness by behaving mischievously. That's just what kids, teens, and adults often do when they feel disconnected to a loved one. And this is especially true for preschoolers who *really* miss their parents after an eight- to twelve-hour separation each day.

• *At the School:* It's valuable if parents can spend a short time at the school to allow their kids time to let go of their day. Bring jeans and a T-shirt to change into after work, so that you are more relaxed and able to play on the playground for a while. Kids like to show off how they've mastered the slide or can stack blocks or build a fort. They like it when they can introduce you to their newest favorite friend and spend a little time playing with them.

Kids then don't feel so rushed, and typically after five to ten minutes, they're ready to go home. And therefore it's more their choice, which dissipates that potential tug-of-war. Plus it helps parents feel more connected with their child's day. You see what they've been most interested in and you know who they've been hanging out with. You also get a chance to bump into some other parents and get to know them a little. All of this feels good to parents with kids of any age and at any level of school.

Also, be sure you don't spend too much time chatting with the teacher. When kids haven't seen their parents all day, the last thing they want is to share your attention with their teacher. I've seen parents in some intense conversations with a teacher while their preschooler is pulling on their pants' leg, whining and clinging away. All the while the parent is putting them off with: "Just a minute, honey . . . I need to talk with Miss Julie." Have the teacher call you at home or work if they need more than a moment with you. Or ask them to write you a note that you can read when your kids are in bed. Kids need and deserve your full attention at the end of the day.

• *Day-care Center to Home:* When the weather is cooperative and it's still light out, stop some days at a park or playground and run around for fifteen to twenty minutes. Or buy some food on the way home and have a picnic. Twenty minutes of going crazy on a playground together is a great way to let go of both your days and reconnect and blow off some steam that you may have accumulated at school or at work.

Bring fun kids' tapes for the car ride. Or maybe a healthy snack surprise. Or let them "read" you their favorite book as you drive. Sing nursery rhymes. Make the ride home fun. If it works out, have your spouse meet you at the park for fun or for your picnic, or one spouse can get home a little earlier and have dinner cooking or ready when the rest of the troop gets home. Doing the unexpected keeps everyone out of a potential negative rut.

Whatever you do, don't try to squeeze in too much on the way home. Stopping at the cleaners and then the grocery store for "just a few things" that turns into a full cart is an invitation for whining and foot-dragging. It's one more potential place for kids to feel like they are being rushed and forced. And it happens to be a time of the day when they are vulnerable to feeling that way. If possible, try to do your chores before you pick up your child. I know a lot of working parents who manage to create a half day or a full day a week off so that they can do most of their shopping, errands, and cleaning, etc., all in one chunk of time without their kids being around.

• *Ahh, Home at Last!:* Once you actually get home, those first thirty minutes will set the tone for the rest of the evening. If you haven't been able to stop and play at a playground, then when you walk through the front door you need to drop everything and take a little time to reconnect. Put on your play clothes; do not listen to phone messages or read the mail or check for E-mails; do not turn on the TV or radio; do not start dinner. First things first: RE-CONNECT! PLAY!

When kids are acting up after being away from you all day, don't get caught in the trap of thinking they just want your attention. It's a deeper feeling than that for kids. It's more a sense of: I miss you. Do you still love me? Am I still important to you? I feel disconnected when I have to share my time with you. They want closeness and love, not just superficial attention.

Kids need your full and undivided love and attention in order to feel close to you and secure again. So go outside and play tag or shoot hoops or kick soccer balls or play in the sand box. Or put on some fun music and dance and sing together. Some kids prefer to curl up in your lap with their favorite book and have some calmer cuddle time. Others prefer to wrestle and be tickled and chased. This focused time together without the distractions (TV, mail, phone, etc.) helps everyone—parents included—feel close and together again. And if your evenings together start with this feeling, you will avoid a lot of potential mischief.

Once you've had your fun together, kids will want to break away and play with their toys. Dad and Mom can then get started on dinner and the wash and the mail. Don't forget to involve your kids in these duties. Let them help you mix and stir and break eggs and set the table and pour drinks. Kids love to be valuable and helpful. Sorting clean clothes is fun for them and another chance to be together with you. Don't underestimate their abilities to be helpful. And don't underestimate the positive feelings that kids receive when they are given opportunities to be valuable and to make a contribution to their home.

• *Express Feelings:* There will be times when you feel out of balance with your work and home responsibilities. Times when you feel tired because you've been lax with taking care of your physical and emotional needs. It's okay to have these feelings, really. But make sure you express them to someone. Don't push them down below the surface or stuff them because they then tend to cause a lot of subconscious mischief (see chapter 2, "Ghosts in the Nursery"). Sometimes you may just need to curl up in your spouse's arms and vent and be heard. You will feel a lot lighter and better about things. And you won't carry the frustration and resentment with you when you are dealing with your kids that causes you to be vulnerable to power struggles and losing it.

Some parents don't feel safe taking these kinds of feelings to their spouse, or don't feel heard and validated by them. So find someone else—your parents, a good friend, a counselor, a support group. It's not easy balancing family life and a career. So be willing to reach out and gather whatever support and resources you need to stay centered, peaceful, and full.

Benefits

As a result of parents proactively taking some of the above steps, everyone will feel more close and secure at the end of the work/school day and thus at the start of their evening together. You really will prevent a lot of the negative attention-getting misbehavior that is a direct result of kids feeling rushed and overpowered and disconnected. Parents will feel good about how they are balancing work and family needs. And a more confident, relaxed parent is a more effective parent when normal mischief arises. You won't get yourself stuck in those unhealthy patterns of power struggles and yelling and frustration.

You will have set a warm, relaxed tone for the rest of your time together before bedtime. Speaking of which, let's move on to that final potential tough time of the day— evening struggles over baths and homework and bedtime.

8

······················

"I Couldn't Get to Sleep at All Last Night!" Putting Evening Power Struggles to Bed!

It's the end of a long day at the Cohen household, and everyone is a bit tired and crabby. Seven-year-old Andy, who was supposed to have taken his bath an hour ago, is camped out in front of the television set.

"Andy, you were supposed to have taken your bath an hour ago! Now it's time for bed!" barks his mom, Ellen.

"Why do I have to take a bath every night?" whines Andy.

"Honey, you always take a bath on school nights. But it's too late now anyway. You can take one in the morning. Let's get ready for bed now."

"I want to finish *Lion King*. It'll be over soon."

"Well, okay, but as soon as it's over you're going right to bed," says Mom. Sure he will.

Twenty minutes later, Mom finds Andy watching a different movie, and her frustration starts to mount.

"I told you that it was bedtime after *Lion King*! Now get going!" Mom yells as she turns off the TV.

Andy heads upstairs, but not before he delivers a mouthful of groaning and complaining. After several reminders from Mom with increasing anger and volume, he finally manages to brush his teeth. When Mom comes in to tuck him in, he's totally engrossed in a major Lincoln Log project. After prying Andy away from the construction site, she reads him a book, that becomes two books, then three. Finally Mom puts her foot down and says, "Lights out!" At that point, the games and demands really begin.

"I'm scared, will you turn on the night-light?"

"I need some water."

"I have to pee!"

Mom and Dad go in and out to argue that there are no monsters to worry about, and he just had a drink, and he just went to the bathroom. But all to no avail. Bedtime was supposed to be at 8:30, and it's already 9:45. And Mom's patience is wearing thin.

"Will you lie with me?" whines Andy in his most forlorn voice.

"Honey, Mommy's tired and needs to go to sleep too. You can fall asleep on your own. You've done it before."

"But I'm scared and I didn't get to see you all day. Stay with me!" begs Andy.

By now at least one of Andy's fish hooks has snared a soft spot in Mom. She has been feeling guilty about the extra hours at work, feeling like she's not been giving her kids enough time.

"Okay, I'll lie here with you, but just for a moment," Mom says without much conviction. Ten minutes later Mom is sound asleep and Andy's still awake, maybe even on the floor knee deep in his toys. She will wake up at two A.M. and notice Andy has fallen asleep amongst his Lincoln Log village. She'll put him in bed, tuck him in, then somehow manage to find her own bed. Eventually she falls asleep, only to be re-awakened at three by the feel of cold little feet on her legs. Andy wants to sleep with her and Dad. Exhausted and in a weakened state, Mom gives in again, but "just for tonight." She will wake up to her alarm at 5:30 A.M., anything but rested. And she'll pay the price for a poor night's sleep all day long.

For some parents, evenings disintegrate into a lot of frustration, which leads to reminding and nagging and yelling. Which results in a not-so-peaceful ending to the family's day. And the pattern repeats itself every night despite the parents' best intentions. So let's get to ways to redirect the mischief at this time of the day.

First off, nighttime is probably not the best time of the day to try to start working on power struggles. It's no accident that werewolves and Dracula did their best work at nighttime. Most parents are tired and have less energy and patience at the end of the day. So it's best to work on the power struggles in the morning and after school first, when you have more patience. Once you've settled those areas, and your kids have learned that you "mean what you say" and that you will follow through with agreements without all the games, then nighttime will be a much easier nut to crack. Because you will have already introduced a new model, a new process for handling issues like getting ready for school in the morning.

When kids are old enough to have a discussion with you, sit down at a peaceful time and make agreements about your evening routine. Make sure to include such items as bathing and brushing teeth (and at what time); reading books (how many, what time you start reading); arranging their room to feel safe (turning on night-lights, closing closet doors, having their favorite toys snuggled in with them). Listen to your children and turn over to them the issue of making their room feel safe. Make sure everyone is crystal clear about the agreements, including what you, the parent, are and are not willing to do. If you have to spend a few extra minutes up front to make sure everyone is on the same page and is clear and has bought into the agreement, it's worth it in order to avoid arguments down the road. Decide as a family to try the new solution for a week or two, then check back with each other about how it's working. Sometimes you may have to tweak things a bit, smooth over a few rough edges. But in general, better cooperation follows if you involve kids in the process.

You might also include in the discussion how you will follow through if they break the agreement. For example, you could tell the kids that if after final tuck-ins they come out of their room asking for you to lie down with them or whatever, that you won't talk to them or argue with them. You'll just calmly and quietly guide them back to their bed and say good night. In other words, don't give them any reasons to keep coming out of their rooms to snare you (hugs, arguing, renegotiating, and lying with them "for just a minute"). For many parents, the first night or two might require them to take little Andy back to his room a few times, complaining and whining all the way. But once he experiences that there are no more games and that his parents follow through with what they said with a new firmness, he'll tend to cooperate pretty quickly.

If you have one of those intense, headstrong kids in your home, it might require a bit more than the above. Some of these kids will "throw the book at you." If they see that their old antics aren't creating the old results (you giving in or playing the game), they will often raise the stakes. In other words, they intensify their mischief which looks like fits that are louder and longer and more intense. It's as if they are saying, "My old tools aren't working. Maybe if I raise the stakes, then I'll get my way."

In this case, you might need to switch to plan B, which requires more serious detachment. In other words, if you hang around too long, it's hard not to get sucked into the fray. Children are good at knowing which buttons to push. As a matter of fact, they are experts at it. So you may need to walk away, saying, "I'm not willing to fight you. We have an agreement. As soon as you are in your bed and quiet, I'll open my door back up. Good night." And with that, walk into your bedroom, close the door, and lock it if you have to. You are telling little Andy, "I am not willing to play the old games of taking you back to your room twenty times. We took the time to make a win-win agreement so I'm just kindly but firmly following through on that agreement."

Now, most intense, combative kids won't like this new tact, so again, be prepared for the worst. I can't tell you how many stories I've heard in my office about kids screaming and hollering outside their parent's bedroom, demanding that they come out. I've had hundreds of kids lie on the floor in the hallway, kicking and pounding the door for long periods, up to an hour or more. And I tell these parents that this is one of their moments of truth. That if they can stay with it, stay detached, stay out of the old games, and really follow though, that their kids will learn some valuable lessons. And it won't take six months. In my experience, it usually takes one or two nights if, and that's a big if, the parents can totally stay out of the games. No arguing, no renegotiating, no anger, no emotion. Just kind but firm follow-through.

Some parents have told me their kids finally fell asleep in the hallway, or after twenty minutes they'd hear them yell from their bedroom, "I'm in my bed now." The parents then opened their door, poked their heads in their child's room and said good night, and it was over. Nirvana.

Now, let me make it clear that I don't really want parents to have to go to their room and close their door on a screaming, out-of-control three year old. It's not my idea of fun. But, if you've given in over and over again and not followed through consistently, at some point you'll probably have to take a stand. And the months or years of not following through often create the need for the major scenes described above.

It's important that you maintain a loving, calm state of mind. The spirit of this is not "I'm sick and tired of your bratty behavior and I've had it!" This conveys a different message, an unhealthy spirit if you will. Detachment does not mean removing your love. It means setting a boundary, physically and/or emotionally. It's remaining the disciplined adult in the situation. It means keeping a cool head, staying calm and present. And loving.

If your child is too young and without enough language to talk through agreements, then your tactics are a bit different. You'll have to decide upon a reasonable evening routine and then let your toddlers know by your simple words and actions. Then follow through, remembering that kind and firm actions speak volumes more than words. The toddler age of eighteen to twenty-four months is a very common time for kids to start bucking bedtime and for waking up at night. (See chapter 3.) It's no surprise that all the turmoil in the daytime carries over into bedtime and nighttime. So it's critical that parents are ready to follow through with their routines and not get sucked into any new games or patterns that they don't want. Like lying with them till they fall asleep, or 2 A.M. snacks, for instance.

Remember my earlier examples about our son John going out in the street and his diaper changes. Those were good examples of how to redirect power struggles with pre-verbal toddlers. Use that same process at bedtime. Follow-through might entail taking them back to their rooms and tuck-ins several times, but without any words or hugs. It might mean poking your head into their room every five or ten minutes because they are screaming and demanding for you to get your buns back in there. Tell them, "I love you, you can fall asleep by yourself, and good night." Then go back to your room. Intense 18-month-olds can be very persistent and won't give it up easily. And, they need to know that all their tantrums will not cause their parents to give in. That is a very unhealthy precedent you set if you end up giving in. Because they've learned that the way to get what they want in life is to be more obnoxious, louder, and more aggressive, they'll take that pattern to the next stage and play havoc with it there too. And so on and so on until their parents at some point decide to toe the line.

For older kids (grade school and above), the same process goes for issues such as homework, time in front of the TV, video and computer games, curfews, and phone time. Sit down with your kids, have a free-for-all discussion about one issue at a time, making sure everyone has lots of say-so. Create a clear, win-win agreement that allows you to follow through in a simple way. Then live it.

The benefits of handling evening power struggles in this manner are many. Most important, kids and parents feel more connected and close at the end of the day as opposed to angry and frustrated. You'll leave your kids each night with warm hugs and warm words. You will have more time for stories and nursery rhymes and snuggling. Parents will naturally feel better about their work-family balance issues, making them more relaxed and confident at both places. It also allows parents more time to take care of their own needs and, God forbid, their marriage needs.

Parents, particularly of young children, tend to neglect both these needs, and the costs to them, their marriage, and ultimately their children are potentially great. Worn-down adults are not going to be calm, effective, loving parents. A home with a crumbling marriage is not a happy, peaceful place for kids to grow up. The state of the marriage is the foundation upon which everything else at home is built. Getting your kids to bed at the right time without all the hassles frees you up to have some quiet time with yourself and your spouse. I can't overemphasize the importance of this time for you and your marriage.

Part 3

The Big Picture: Putting It All Together

9

....

Oh, by the Way . . . Other Important Contributing Factors

We've talked along the way about how factors such as temperament, ghosts in the nursery, and developmental stages affect a child's behavior and how parents parent. Let's briefly discuss the potential effects of a couple of other important factors.

SEPARATION/DIVORCE: POTENTIAL EFFECTS ON PARENTS AND KIDS

• *Distraction:* Parents who are experiencing problems with their spouse, and especially if those problems lead to separation or divorce, have a lot on their minds—and even more important—in their hearts. They go through an emotional roller coaster, feeling everything from anger and resentment to loneliness, disappointment, fear, sadness, hurt, and confusion. This makes it very difficult for them to be emotionally available for their kids.

Kids sense these emotions and their parents' distraction and distance, and in some way react to them. Some kids get quiet and withdrawn, others become angry and mischievous. Frequent fits and outbursts are typical, increasing the potential for power struggles. Kids decide at a subconscious level that even if the connection to their parents during the struggles is negative (involving arguments and yelling), that connection is better than none. Better than feeling distant. So parents have to really be on their toes and on top of themselves and the mischief. And they have to take care of their emotional needs and their grieving so that when they are with their kids they are really present and able to hear *all* of their children's feelings. Parents whose cups are full have the energy and patience and love to be there for their children in their times of need.

• *Guilt:* Most parents feel guilty about the pain and changes they are causing for their kids. Many times this guilt leads them to being more permissive, to give in more, to loosen up the boundaries. Thus, they create some of those unhealthy patterns we've been talking about in previous chapters.

• *Two Households with Two Sets of Rules:* This scenario often creates a potential for power struggles because it's a place for kids to push boundaries. "I can do that at Mom's house!" It's also pretty confusing for kids, especially younger ones, to have to understand the differences in rules in two homes. And when you add in parents' girlfriends and boyfriends, and then stepmoms and stepdads, the discipline issues can get really confusing and complicated. And therefore there is more room for kids to push and manipulate and send parents into power struggles.

• *Kids' Emotions:* Kids going through a divorce end up on a similar emotional roller coaster as their parents. And we know that when kids feel hurt and disconnected they are much more likely to get into mischief. Kids also feel powerless, a loss of control. They had no say-so in whether or not their parents got divorced, or where they live and when. And when kids (or adults) feel a loss of control in their lives, they look for ways to get a sense of control back. If parents don't provide healthy ways to feel powerful, kids tend to get that feeling by engaging people in power struggles, because it does give them a sense of control. They push buttons and adults jump.

ATTENTION DEFICIT DISORDER (ADD)/LEARNING DISABILITIES (LD)

When kids have a hard time sitting still, focusing, and remembering directions, parents aren't sure that these kids *can* understand their discipline. So they go into situations with kids less sure of themselves, more hesitant, more ambivalent, more apt to give in. And if you mix a power-hungry kid with an ambivalent parent, you get power struggles.

So it pays for parents to break things down into manageable pieces. And it pays to get help from professionals like teachers, psychologists, and speech therapists. Teachers and therapists can give parents specific feedback about exactly what their child can or can't understand and put together as far as directions and directives and boundaries. They can tell parents whether their child's cognitive and language development allows them to understand and cooperate within their discipline and limits. Armed with this information, parents can approach discipline situations more clearly and confidently because they have teased apart what their child "can't do" versus what they "won't do." And as we've learned, a clear, confident parent is a more effective parent.

DEPRESSED PARENTS

Research has shown that even 3-month-old babies who have lived with a depressed mom act a lot differently. These babies already have different expectations about their caretakers; they react with more anger and withdrawal when their emotional needs aren't met. As they get to the preschool years these kids tend to have poor impulse control, more anger, and less ability to monitor their emotions. They have a hard time connecting to kids and adults. And they, therefore, are more apt to act out and engage people in power struggles.

And as mentioned before, if children feel disconnected from a depressed parent, they will usually prefer any kind of connection or attention to none at all. And that pattern of engaging parents at home tends to carry over to all adults eventually. These kids learn to connect to others through mischief.

PARENTS WHO DISAGREE ON DISCIPLINE

We learned in chapter 4 how preschoolers are experts at manipulation and stirring things up. And what more fertile ground can there be but two parents who disagree on discipline? Kids learn to play one parent against the other. They learn to distract parents from the real issue, their mischief, and to instead focus on arguing with each other. It can create less consistent follow-through and more confusion because the boundaries aren't clear. To anyone!

When parents can face their kids with a united front, especially when it comes to following through on agreements, a ton of hassle is avoided. Parents don't have to agree on everything. But it pays for them to talk through issues before they approach their kids so that they can at least be on the same page. If situations get a little heated, it is okay for a parent to take a time-out, to cool off and get their act together with their spouse. They then can come back to the situation with the kids in a calm, confident tone. That way you can keep your emotions, especially frustration and anger, out of the situation, making you again much more effective.

I have found that parents with different ideas about parenting often criticize each other, e.g., "She's too permissive," or, "He's too strict and rigid." This criticism tends to push the other parent further to their corner, to an extreme position in many cases. The permissive parent feels sorry for her kids because her spouse has been so critical, so she feels the need to be easier on the kids to balance out her spouse, and vice versa. If the parents can go to a parenting class together or read parenting books together and have some open discussions about how they can support each other in their parenting, everyone wins. They may still disagree on some issues, but they've come to the middle to a place where they can agree to disagree yet still be supportive of each other. And at this point, their kids no longer can stir up the old parent versus parent mischief.

10

·················

What to Do When . . .

I have been asked a lot of questions in my office, during parenting classes, during seminars, and on my call-in radio show by working parents. So I thought this would be a good time in this book to discuss how to handle specific problem situations that many working parents face. The following are questions asked by real-life parents. Their names have been changed to protect the exhausted!

PARENTS WHO WORK AT HOME

What do you do when . . . your kids keep interrupting your work?

First of all, make sure that you have spent plenty of time playing with your kids at non-working times. If you're distracted or preoccupied with work matters when you're been with them, your kids may feel disconnected from you, left out, or not important. They then might create a lot of negative attention-getting behavior to wake you up and get you to engage them. So sit down and eat meals with them while keeping the phone off the hook, the newspaper folded away, and the TV off. When you are with them, give them 100 percent of your focus so they feel important, heard, and loved.

Maybe you could break for lunch twenty minutes early in order to go outside and play with the kids. After your workday, close the office door and turn the recorder on. If you *have* to make some return calls, set aside a block of time in the evening to do so as opposed to answering calls off and on all evening.

Many work-at-home parents have told me that things improved when they moved their home office to the basement or another room away from the main house activities. Kind of the out-of-sight, out-of-mind mentality. Also, the less they had to venture upstairs to get a cup of coffee or a snack or supplies, the less interruptions they got from their kids. Put your coffee machine and snacks in your office space. If you were in an office building and had to make frequent trips to the coffee machine, copy machine, or fax, you'd waste a lot of time chatting with co-workers too.

With young children, it's usually best not to see them during the hours you are working. See them at lunch, but otherwise avoid contact that might cause them to start whining or clinging again. On days where you *really* need uninterrupted, focused time, have the sitter take your kids out of the house to the park or a movie.

Be clear with your sitter that you are *not* to be interrupted. If a toddler knows that a huge fit can sometimes get them an audience with you, they'll keep pushing those buttons. Beyond emergencies, you are off-limits and the sitter is entrusted to handle all issues that come up.

Adopt a personal routine whereby when you are at work, you are fully at work. And when you are with your family, you are fully present and attentive to them. You can sneak in some work time in the evenings when your kids are doing *their* homework. Maybe take your laptop or work to the table where they are doing homework so you can answer their occasional questions. Have some fun time together before bedtime, playing board games or reading books. Once you've tucked them in, you can go back to your office and get any extra work done.

And just know that when you are dealing with preschoolers, there are going to be some occasional rough days when for whatever reason they are just out of sorts. On those days, take your work to the local library, or have the sitter take the kids out of the house. That is one disadvantage to working at home. But for most parents, the advantages far outweigh the disadvantages. You have more time at home with your children. Mornings are much less rushed and harried. Work hours are more flexible. You avoid a lot of wasted time driving in rush hour or chatting with coworkers.

WEEKEND WORK AT HOME

What do you do when . . . you have to get some office work done on the weekend and your kids are wanting you to be with them?

Some parents avoid this hassle by either doing their work early or late in the day. They find they can get a ton of work done between 5 and 8 A.M. or after 10 P.M. when everyone else is asleep. Or they sneak in a couple of good hours during naptime or when their spouse takes the kids out for a couple of hours of shopping or errands or visiting friends and relatives.

Or do what I described in the last section—hole up for a block of uninterrupted time. You can explain your situation and needs to kids who are old enough to understand. Let them know how much time you need for your work, and what time you'll be available to play with them. When that time arrives, drop whatever you're doing and keep your commitment with them. Kids hate being put off with lots of "just a few more minutes" that stretch into hours.

And, if you are getting frustrated and resentful about how much work you're taking home as opposed to how little time you have to spend with your spouse and kids, maybe it's time to reconsider your job, or your line of work. Decide how much time you want to spend with your family, then make whatever tough decisions you need to make to create what you want. And do it now, because kids grow up so fast. Remember that famous quote that reads: no one ever says on their deathbed that they wished they had spent more time at the office.

GRANDMA'S HOUSE

What do you do when . . . kids try to pull power struggles with Grandma or Aunt Barbara?

Some kids go to a relative's house for their day care. For this arrangement to work out, it's important that Grandma be up to speed with the child's stage and potential mischief. Parents should relay to Grandma what their child has been up to lately, and especially what has worked for them as far as redirecting any power struggles.

A grandmother called in on my radio show recently with a question about a grandson she babysits. It seemed that no matter what kind of food she put before him, he'd refuse to eat it because "it wasn't what Mommy and Daddy make for me." She had tried to make him sit at the table until he ate his food, but had seen this ploy deteriorate into a major power struggle.

I suggested that she disengage from the struggle and let go of how much he ate. Get suggestions from the parents about foods he likes and put them out in front of him. If he eats, great. If not, that's fine too. After a reasonable amount of time, take the food away and say, "Lunch is over," and go on with your day. If he's hungry, he'll eventually let go of the struggle, but only if his grandma lets go first, so that there is no tug-of-war.

The same goes for other issues: Grandma needs to learn not to engage her grandson in these battles, and to stay kind, loving and firm. Now, if grandparents only see kids for occasional visits, I think any "spoiling" or loosening of boundaries is fine. It's part of the fun of being a grandparent, and it's a huge bonus for kids to develop a trusting, special relationship with them. But this does not hold true if grandparents are the regular, daily sitter. I think this requires the parents and grandparents to have a lot of conversations about how the parents want their child to be parented. Grandparents need to respect this because they are spending so much time with the kids and therefore need to be on the same wavelength as the parents so as to not confuse the child and to be supportive of the parents.

If parents are not happy with the way they were raised and don't want their kids to be grandparented that way, then either educate the grandparents or find a different sitter. Otherwise, you've added a major stressor to your day—a power struggle with your parents. Give Grandma this book to read, take a parenting seminar or class together. If Grandma can come around to your way of thinking, what a gift for your child to have so much undivided time with their grandparents.

SIBLING FIGHTS

What do you do when . . . siblings start in on each other in the car on the way home from school?

First off, review my suggestions from chapter 7 on the day-care center to home transition. Make sure you haven't rushed or overpowered your kids out the door. Those few moments spent allowing kids to transition to your care are invaluable. Give them some choice about who sits where in the car. Surprise them with snacks or a fun tape or book they can read to you. Let someone be the seat belt monitor to be sure everyone is buckled in before you drive off. Remember that kids who feel connected, heard, important, and valuable don't need to get into mischief.

At a non-conflict time, for instance at a family meeting, you can discuss this issue of how to handle sibling disagreements in the car. This will make it easier for you to act quickly and be more detached when fights pop up. Let your kids know that you will be unwilling to drive if they are yelling or arguing, thus making it hard or dangerous for you to drive safely. Tell them you will ask them to quiet down, and if they continue, that you will find the first safe side street or parking lot and pull over until they can quiet down. When you pull over to the side of the road safely, either have them get out of the car until they can handle their squabble, or you can step outside. Obviously, this needs to be a safe spot.

I remember one winter we were pulling out of the driveway to go on a New Year's Eve family weekend. Our then 7-year-old Kelly and 5-year-old T.J. started arguing about who got to hold the new puppy. We told them to step outside the car, and they could come back in as soon as they had the seating arrangements handled for the whole trip. Just a moment or two later they said they were ready to go, and my wife and I questioned if they were sure they had the whole trip figured out. They proceeded to give us a blow-by-blow description of who was to sit where and who could hold the dog when. We said, "Great job guys. Let's get going," and the rest of our three-hour trip was peaceful.

Now you have to be willing to wait them out. This is another of those situations where you are again training your kids that you mean what you say and that you'll follow through no matter what. But you'll only have to do this a time or two, and then you are done with it. Whenever they start getting too loud, just ask them if you need to pull over, and they'll quickly tell you, "No, no, we'll quiet down." So I'm encouraging you to put the time in for this training, no excuses. If you are a little late to something a time or two it is worth it in the long run because then you won't have to hassle with it or worry about it happening every day.

HOMEWORK HASSLES

What do you do when . . . it takes three hours of coaxing and pleading and nagging to get your child to do their homework?

The homework issue can really create a lot of tension and frustration in the evenings if you let it, especially if parents take on too much responsibility. When parents of grade schoolers tell me, "*We* have to spend hours at the table to finish the work," I immediately correct them by pointing out that it's their child's homework, not theirs. They've already graduated from grade school, so keep the ball in their child's court where it belongs.

I think that kids should view their schoolwork as their responsibility right from the start, in kindergarten. Obviously, kids need more help in the first few years to get organized and to do the work, and it is imperative that parents have the intention of slowly but surely backing away from the issue so that by third grade, kids are really in charge. It's much easier to accomplish this letting-go process in early grade school than it will be in middle and high school, where the consequences are much greater and parents' influence and control is much less.

Once again, this issue can be discussed at a family meeting. Brainstorm about when they want to do their homework, where is the best spot to do it, and how their parents are willing to be involved. Maybe the parents are willing to give one reminder at the agreed upon time, or maybe the parents and child decide together that the child would like to be able to play after school up until dinnertime, and then do their homework right after dinner before anything else (phone calls, TV, video games). If the child doesn't start into his homework after dinner, the parents should kindly but firmly remind him of the agreement and follow through on not allowing anything else to happen until it's done. Don't argue; don't renegotiate; don't get angry. Just follow through.

Let kids know that if they have legitimate questions, you of course will help them figure it out, but that you will *not* be willing to sit there by their side for two hours and in essence do it for them. And you will *not* care about finishing it more than they do. Whenever I see parents more invested in schoolwork than their kids, I know I'll find an unmotivated kid who requires a lot of reminding, threatening, punishments, and rewards to get them going. And this is the main culprit when homework power struggles abound in a home.

Working parents are more vulnerable to getting sucked into doing too much for many reasons. Many parents feel guilty about being gone so much, so they overdo things like homework and science projects and pinewood derby cars and batting cages. This overinvolvement serves to make them feel better about all the times when maybe they couldn't be there for a class play or a soccer game.

Many working parents end up feeling a little out of touch with their children's lives too, not knowing classroom friends, current school projects, or their child's coaches and teammates' parents. So they react with too much control and concern when they do get involved to make up for lost time. And if a student can get their parents to take responsibility for homework or a project, they'll gladly pass the buck. Kids who forget a lot usually have parents who remind and nag a lot. And this does not serve them in the long run, because they don't learn to be self-motivated, responsible students. This will catch up to them by middle and high school.

In summary, parents should go into the whole school issue with the intention that they are there to support and encourage, not motivate and do for their kids. Create win-win agreements about all the schoolwork issues so that everyone is clear about what is expected from each person. Then follow through without any arguing or frustration. Parents can keep up with their child's progress by checking worksheets and tests that come home in folders, keeping in touch with teachers by being involved as a classroom helper as often as they can manage it, and by making school functions such as parent-teacher nights and parties. Your involvement with the classroom sends a message that you care about their education and are on top of things as far as school goes.

This means that sometimes, you'll have to allow kids to

experience some natural consequences. If they forget an assignment, they may get a zero or have to stay in at recess to complete it. Let the teacher work those things out with your child without having to involve you. Some parents I've worked with who waited until middle or high school to let go of this responsibility had to allow their teens to fail for a quarter in order to show that they really weren't going to jump in and rescue them or take charge. Again, it's harder to do this with a sophomore than with a third grader.

HOSTAGES

What do you do when . . . your three year old is holding the family hostage?

Remember the example from the beginning of chapter 4 where Tyler would not allow his family to go out for pizza (his sister Mariah's suggestion) by throwing a tantrum? Since I see hundreds of Tylers in my office, I'm often asked how I would handle the situation differently. Here's my answer:

First and foremost, if I know I have a strong-minded, intense, power-hungry 3-year-old, my first job is to be sure I'm doing everything in my power to give him power in appropriate ways (see Healthy, Effective Parenting for the Stage of Identity in chapter 4). Never underestimate or forget the importance of this preventative step. If I've done a good job of finding more and more ways to empower him in situations all day long, I probably can avoid these big confrontations.

Second, I can set up some teaching moments by planning ahead a bit. Call a nearby sitter and ask if he or she would be available tonight at dinner time for an hour or so in case you need them. This step is crucial because you don't want your boundary setting and limit setting to be idle threats with no teeth. Then I'd have a short and sweet heart-to-heart talk with Tyler. I'd let him know that if he throws a fit before we go out to dinner or refuses to get dressed or get into the car, etc., that you will have a sitter come over to watch him while the rest of the family goes out to eat. Let him know that he won't get two chances. Then drop it.

When the time to decide on a dining spot is at hand, create a win-win situation as best you can. If you've given in to him the past several times and it is Mariah's turn to choose, then let her choose. If Tyler pitches a fit and refuses to get dressed to go, immediately detach from the struggle and call the sitter. Tyler will be shocked when the sitter walks through the front door. And if he's like most kids he'll quickly turn angelic and plead that "I'll get dressed now, I want to go with you." At that moment, it's the parent's job to say, "I'm sorry, you missed out on your chance to get ready and now it's too late. We'll try again next time we're going out to dinner. We'll see you later." Give him a hug if he'll let you, then calmly leave. If he flips out, let him flip. It's just his way to try to get you to reconsider.

Make sure you don't make any snide or disrespectful comments on your way out. Comments like, "Maybe *now* you'll learn your lesson," or, "We're sick of your Mickey Mouse behavior. We're outta here!" You want to stay loving, kind, firm, and matter-of-fact. You're not angry or frustrated because he no longer has the power to make you feel upset. You've taken that power back to where it belongs. *You* are in charge of your emotions and will no longer react when he pushes buttons.

And again, in my experience, it will take one or two incidents like this in order for Tyler to understand his parents mean it and there are no longer any games or give in the system. He'll be much more respectful and cooperative with this issue from then on. It will be a non-issue. If you couple this with other experiences where you employ immediate kind and firm follow-through, then Tyler and your home will settle down in a matter of weeks.

If you come back from your dinner out and find out Tyler had a great time with the sitter, all the better. You are not trying to make him suffer in order to learn his lesson. The lesson is that his parents mean business with their boundaries and won't allow his escalating antics to cause them to cave in to his wishes. It's also a matter of taking care of yourself as parents. Who wants to walk into a restaurant with a half-naked 3-year-old with an attitude who might lose it at any moment and ruin your evening, again?

Much of our discipline as kids approach the teen years is about taking care of ourselves, respecting ourselves and our home. You can't *make* a 17-year-old not drink when they go out on Friday night, but you *can* take care of your car and home and the younger kids by having clear, firm boundaries regarding use of the family car and not allowing alcohol and drugs and cigarettes in your home. So this example with a 3-year-old is the start of that process that will take parents through the teen years.

COMMUNICATING WITH SITTERS AND TEACHERS

What do you do when . . . sitters or teachers get involved with these power struggles?

The best way to handle this is to keep the lines of communication open between you and them. If you are working on ironing out the morning wrinkles, call the day-care teacher and tell her what you are up to. Let her know your little darling may be coming to school in her pajamas for a few days until you get over the hump with this power struggle area. I've never had a teacher not be supportive of parents during these endeavors.

If you are working on turning over more responsibility to kids for their schoolwork, have a *parent-teacher-student conference* and come up with a plan together. Let the teacher know that if there is an assignment missing, they are to talk with your child, not you. You can work out how to stay in touch with the teacher in order to check in occasionally on their progress. What you want to avoid is having to sign things or check things every day that causes you to get too involved in making sure your child succeeds and sets you up for struggles.

If you have a sitter come to your house or use a home day care, explain to the caregiver what you are experiencing as far as your child's behavior and what steps you are taking to prevent or redirect it. Let them know what has worked for you and maybe they can fill you in on what has worked for them. It becomes a supportive two-way partnership. The same goes for a teacher as well. It still amazes me how seldom teachers from the previous school year pass on gold nuggets of what worked for them with a challenging kid to next year's teacher. What a waste of valuable information.

Best case, Cadillac model, would be that you and your child's caregiver go to a parenting class together, read the same books, and have a running dialogue to be sure you are supporting each other's efforts. I have seen excellent success stories in this regard when parents came to my parenting class with a nanny or a grandparent or sitter. A united front is important when dealing with challenging toddlers.

DESPERATION CALLS

What do you do when . . . you get phone calls at work about or from distraught kids?

Phone calls in the middle of your workday can be very distracting and frustrating. Sometimes kids will call in tears because their older sibling is "torturing" them. Sometimes they'll be screaming at you because you won't let them ride their bike to a friend's house. These calls are never pretty and they usually leave the parent feeling powerless, frustrated, and guilty. Powerless and frustrated because there rarely is much that you can do to make things better. Guilty because parents have a hard time not questioning whether or not it's worth the effort to work outside the home if it's going to be this hard.

Once again, family meetings can come to your rescue, because this is yet another issue that can be discussed together as a family at a quiet time. Set up routines for after school that will work for everyone. This might include calling when they walk in the door to check in with you. Maybe you could chat for just a few moments to hear highlights from their day and to talk about your reunion that evening.

As part of this discussion, be clear about your boundary that they are to handle their disagreements themselves or wait until you get home. They are not to call you at work for that sort of problem, but only for emergencies. If you have a sitter who watches the kids for those after-school hours before you get home, include them in this discussion so that they also know they aren't to call you except for emergencies. You've already given them information on how to handle the kids as in the above mentioned example. If you can't entrust your sitter with this kind of responsibility, maybe you need to find a more competent sitter. A competent sitter will give you more peace of mind and thus a more focused workday.

I remember a family in my office a few months ago who had 13- and 15-year-old boys, John and Joe respectively, who were always on each other. Both parents worked full-time jobs and were getting numerous panicky phone calls from the 13-year-old complaining about his brother. For years the pattern had been that the parents rescued poor John and blamed and punished Joe. This made Joe feel resentful and angry, and he got back at his brother whenever his parents weren't looking and especially after school when he and John were alone. I spoke with the parents about how to take a different stance as far as their role in the fights (see Sibling Fights, page 143), and also to the boys about the costs of each maintaining their position in this vicious cycle. After three visits, I concluded that neither of the boys was willing to let go of the fight for now, so that their parents needed to take action to take care of themselves. This looked like getting a sitter on some days, and John staying at an after-school program the other days until they could settle the issues. The boys had proven that they weren't old enough or mature enough yet to take care of themselves without the parents present.

Bottom line: Make it clear that you are not to be called at work for silly and inconsequential situations. If kids know they can get you engaged in inappropriate arguments and discussions, they will keep calling. Remember too that sometimes these inappropriate phone calls are a child's way of saying, "Hello, I miss you! I feel disconnected from you because of how busy and rushed our family has been lately. And I need more closeness with you."

GOOD-BYE SCENES

What do you do when . . . your youngster has major drama scenes at your separation times?

Those separation scenes at day-care centers can certainly be brutal for kids, parents, and teachers alike. But they don't have to be. There are many things that you can do to prevent these disasters. The following are some suggestions:

First, if you've put into practice my suggestions from chapter 6, you should be experiencing calm, non-rushed mornings. When you can get off to a good start whereby everyone feels loved and empowered, that is the best preventative medicine for avoiding tough separation scenes. Even if your child is going through a stage when they have normal separation anxiety, it still makes things a lot smoother if parents and kids have had time to connect in the mornings. Parents feel more confident and less guilty, so they won't add any undue anxiety to the child's plate.

Be sure that on the way to school you don't harp on the separation issue. The parents I see who go on and on about how "Daddy will miss them" and "You'll be fine today" create more anxiety in their kids, not less. I'd rather see you sing nursery rhymes or tell stories together all the way to school. When you arrive, be sure you've allowed yourself an extra few minutes to get your toddler settled in.

Some kids can be dropped off at the door and they never even look back. Others may require a little last minute TLC. Walk into school holding hands; maybe help them hang up their coat; and find a friend who's already started building a tower of blocks. Get on their level, give them a hug, tell them you can't wait to see them after school and hear about all their adventures, then calmly get up and leave. If they start to cry, the teacher can take over from there. And almost always, the fussing lasts for only a few moments, and then you are quickly forgotten as they get involved with friends and activities.

Don't make it a long, drawn-out affair because that makes *both* of you feel worse. Be understanding, loving, and detached. Detached, meaning keep your emotions out of it at this point. If you need to cry, wait until you get to your car and then call a friend or have a good cry alone. Be more matter-of-fact at the good-bye scene so your kids don't pick up on any of your feelings of guilt, anxiety, or sadness.

If the above doesn't help the separation problems to resolve, you might need to go see someone like me to talk the issue through. There may be an important "ghost" that is interfering. Sometimes parents just need reassurance that their child is normal and that they are good parents in order to relax. Do whatever it takes, because a prolonged period of dramatic separation anxiety and rough scenes can really undermine a parent's confidence and cause undue confusion about working outside the home.

"I'M SPENT!"

What do you do when . . . you have no energy left at the end of the day or week for your family?

Peggy came to see me because of frustration and confusion about her work-family balance. And she was exhausted. In order for her to get the job advance she wanted she needed to be at work a couple of evenings a week and do work on the weekends too. There was a lot of chaos and mischief going on in her office, and she felt unsupported by her boss. At home, her husband wasn't much help with the kids, and once a month he left for a long weekend in the Reserves. So she felt unsupported at home as well. Her 6-year-old son and 3-year-old daughter were out of control and uncooperative, leaving Mom feeling drained most evenings.

"I have good intentions every weekend," she told me, "but by the time I do the grocery shopping, laundry, and house cleaning, I have no energy left for the kids. I feel terrible because during the week I always promise that we'll do things together on the weekends, but we rarely get to them. As for time for my marriage or, God forbid, time for me, what a joke!"

I helped Peggy see that part of her dilemma was due to her inability to set good boundaries for herself with her husband and kids. We discussed ways to involve the whole family in household duties so that she wasn't doing it all on her own. She also figured out a way that she could get an hour's worth of exercise in three times a week that wouldn't throw off the rest of her life. She could create more time and energy for herself also by avoiding the morning (see chapter 6) and bedtime (see chapter 8) power struggles. If you can nestle your children all snug in their beds by 8:00 or 8:30 that extra hour or two can be used for all kinds of goodies.

Perhaps even more important, I helped Peggy see that she was miserable in her present job, mostly due to the unhealthy relationships there. I remember seeing her a year later, and she was in good spirits. She had quit her former job and was now working four days per week in a new small company where she felt appreciated and supported. She used that extra day off to do her running around and house-work so that she was more present when she was with her kids. I suggested she also use some of her day off to do some activities that would nourish and refresh her, give her energy, refuel her.

Peggy was able to create a job for herself that gave her the time and flexibility she needed in order to balance work and household responsibilities. I encourage you to do the same. Your children deserve to grow up in a home where their parents have time to play with them. They need lots of special one-on-one time, and leisurely quiet time together. Marriages require the same kind of nurturing and so do individual parents. If parents don't take good care of them-selves as individuals and as a couple, it will be next to impossible to be the effective parents they wish to be. It just won't happen because crabby, impatient, tired, drained adults don't do well with power-hungry, mischievious kids of all ages. Especially if the kids are crabby and tired from a long day at day care. Or from a full day of grade school plus two hours of after-school care. It's a combustible mix-ture to say the least.

I guess part of my message with this issue is to take stock of your life. Make some tough decisions about your career if you need to. There may be some concessions to your career, but they'll more than be made up for by in-creased closeness at home.

11

·················

The Big Picture: Putting It All Together

This book has given you a chance to look at parenting for the long-term. Sometimes it's easier to nag or yell or overpower kids in order to get them to do what you want. Or you may think it's easier to give in, in order to avoid a conflict or a tantrum. But in the long run, you are creating more problems for yourself and your kids. You end up with more power struggles, more fits, and a child who feels that "the world owes me a living." A child who has learned that the way for him to get what he wants is to be more obnoxious and willful. And *that* pattern will hurt them in all of their future relationships, with peers and adults.

Let's review for a moment what we've learned about redirecting and preventing these common power struggles.

First, remember all the reasons why kids and parents might butt heads in the mornings, after school, and in the evenings. Remember the importance that a child's temperament plays in this area. More intense, resistant, stubborn kids will take these struggles a lot further than more easygoing kids. They tend to bring more emotion and more intensity to their important stages, making it more difficult for parents to stay detached.

DEVELOPMENTAL STAGES

Understanding that it is normal and important for kids to try to engage adults in power struggles helps parents stay out of them. It is a young child's job, their mandate, to push buttons for all of the developmental reasons discussed in chapters 3, 4, and 5. This quest for control helps kids learn about boundaries, how to ask for what they want, and to be aware of their power. Knowing about these stages ahead of time really helps parents to normalize their children's behavior and not take it personally. Anticipatory guidance can prevent a lot of unnecessary power struggles.

GOODWILL ACCOUNT

One of the most important influences on how effective parents are at getting cooperation at home is the state of their "Goodwill Account." By Goodwill Account I mean how does the relationship feel between the parent and child. If the parents have been making regular deposits (listening, respecting, giving say-so, spending special time together, showing appreciation) and the "account" is full, then the relationship feels safe, respectful, trusting, close, and loving. And when there is that kind of feeling going on between people, then it is easy to create win-win solutions, hold each other accountable, and be flexible.

If, on the other hand, the parents have been making a lot of withdrawals from the account (yelling, nagging, criticizing, spanking, breaking their word), then the account becomes low. When the account is low, the relationship feels unsafe, disrespectful, tense, and distant. And at this point it's much harder to gain cooperation and to communicate with each other, because there is just not enough "goodwill" in the relationship.

So it pays to take preventative measures by making regular deposits into the Goodwill Account.

GHOSTS IN THE NURSERY

We all bring a lot of past beliefs and experiences into our parenting. Being aware of these old feelings and beliefs allows them to remain conscious. And if those ghosts in the nursery are up on the table for us to see and keep in mind, then we have control over them and can do something about them. We're in charge of them instead of them influencing us in unhealthy ways.

DISCOURAGED OR DISCONNECTED KIDS

One of the main reasons kids get into these patterns of misbehavior (besides parents not understanding and thus plugging in to normal developmental stages); is that kids feel disconnected. Kids who feel disconnected from parents, kids who feel hurt or not heard, and kids who feel overpowered often react to these feelings by getting into mischief. The mischief can create some kind of connection with parents, and as we've all heard a million times before, negative attention is better than none. Pushing boundaries and playing tug-of-war with adults also gives kids a tremendous sense of control and power. It's inappropriate, but it's better than feeling powerless.

If you've ever left young children for a trip away with your spouse, you'll know what I'm talking about. Remember how little kids seem to "pay us back" when we return home. We're expecting some joyous reunion, and we get the cold shoulder and a lot of mischief for about a day. And it's because they've been feeling sad and disconnected because of missing us.

Or think about kids who come from a divorced family. When they've been staying with the other parent for a few days and then return to their other home, that parent will often experience what the vacationers above experienced. Mischief for a while until everyone can reconnect and get back to their schedule and rhythm together.

LESSONS KIDS LEARN DUE TO THEIR PARENTS' NEW, EFFECTIVE APPROACH

• **The world is a safe place, and I feel safe and secure.** Having clear, consistent boundaries does give kids this sense of security and especially during those stages when they are emotionally (and physically) bouncing off the walls.

• **It is good to be powerful.** When children are given lots of opportunities to have power and control in appropriate ways at home, they learn to be more responsible and independent. They learn to use power appropriately and how to ask for what they want in effective ways so that they get more of what they want in life. So many of us parents never learned that growing up, and it haunts us today. It created adults who have a hard time knowing what they want and asking for what they want in their relationships; who have a hard time setting emotional and physical boundaries; who don't know who they are or where they are going or what their dream and purpose are. This results in a lot of unhappy, divorced, angry, resentful, and depressed grown-ups. Let's do it differently with the next generation.

• **I have a lot of say-so in my home.** Involving kids in the agreement-making-process is so empowering for them, as little kids and later as teens. You really are preparing your family for the teen years by giving kids input today as preschoolers. It's a healthy, long-term model for gaining cooperation at home or in a classroom (or in a business boardroom). And what a gift it is to know how to create win-wins with people you are close to. They will use these skills with their friends, dates, and eventually spouses and employees.

• **My parents mean what they say.** It is essential for a child's long-term happiness that they learn that they will be held accountable to their agreements and their word; that they are responsible for their actions and decisions; that throwing fits and being angry or intimidating won't get them what they want or get their parents to give in. Those can be such unhealthy patterns to bring into the school setting with teachers or onto the playground with peers. No one will want to be friends with a kid who is always bossy, a bully, or overpowering. You'll be saving your child a lot of unnecessary heartache if you can nip those patterns when they are younger.

• **My parents follow through on our agreements without any "games."** This saves us all a lot of wasted energy arguing, reminding, manipulating, and yelling. Everyone knows where they stand and what is expected of them. Agreements and follow-through are clear and done in a kind but firm manner which feels respectful. There are no double standards or "do as I say, not as I do" issues.

• **I feel more loved and calm because my family has lots of time to play and have fun instead of wasting time on all the old monkey business.** Issues are handled quickly with no fuss and no mess, leaving more time for togetherness.

LESSONS PARENTS LEARN BECAUSE OF THIS NEW MODEL

• **My kids feel more happy, calm, secure, and empowered when I follow through on agreements and hold firm on my boundaries.** And that is the fuel that should make it easier for parents to continue having clear, firm boundaries all the way through the teen years even when they are "the only parents in the whole school who won't let their 16 year old go unsupervised to Cancun over spring break!" Kids can be pretty dramatic and look pretty miserable when they don't always get their way and especially during the egocentric preschool and teenage years. It helps if parents are comfortable and secure with their boundary setting before the going gets tough. And the costs climb higher as their kids get older.

• **By giving kids a lot of say-so in the agreement process, I gain more cooperation and take on less responsibil-**

ity for the running of the home. This prevents a ton of resentment that many parents feel today, because they are doing too much at home. This is especially true for working parents who feel they are burning the candle from both ends and because they've taken on too much. That's their fault, not their kids. It frees up parents to have more time for fun and play with their kids. And to feel more light, less heavy and angry all the time.

• **By detaching and letting go I am a more effective parent.** This is one of the hardest things for a parent to learn. And yet there are so many chances for them to practice in the early years before the stakes are so high and scary (drugs, sex, driving). When they see how much more effective they are at handling their 18-month-old's temper tantrum when they can keep their emotions out of it, it gives parents more confidence for the next time they need to detach and unplug.

• **I recognize the stages of my child's development, and as a result can better support my child during this period.** Parents gain confidence both in themselves and in their children as they successfully support their kids in navigating through developmental transitions in a detached but effective manner. When parents can step back from all the emotions it's much easier to see the behavior for what it is, to see the benefits the child gains from mastering each stage, to not take any of the child's behaviors personally. When parents can support their child in this way through a tough stage, it makes it easier for parents to do the same for the next transition, because they trust the process, trust their child to get through it with valuable lessons learned, and trust themselves to be the loving support they want to be for their kids.

• **By revisiting my ghosts I can separate my feelings from my child's behavior.** Not only do parents have an opportunity to see their children in a deeper light with each new transition, they also get a chance to see themselves differently as well. Parents are pushed at each stage to search and be aware of their own feelings that are provoked due to their child's behavior. When these emotions are conscious, it's a great time for parents to get some counseling or go on a retreat to do some soul searching in order to deal with their emotions. If they can effectively work through their feelings, hopefully they can put their ghosts to rest.

BEGINNING WITH THE END IN MIND

This is one of Stephen Covey's Seven Habits of Highly Effective People and Families. And it fits so well with the theme in *Food Fights and Bedtime Battles*. Every parent I've ever met wants to raise kids who become teens and finally adults who are responsible, happy, loving, and self-motivated; adults who know how to create healthy relationships where everyone has a voice and power, where cooperation and win-wins are routine, where closeness and integrity and fun are the most important values in the home.

Parents can achieve all the above if they get a good start with learning to deal with young children in effective ways, and if they can establish positive, healthy models for gaining cooperation and handling conflicts. Kids deserve to grow up in a home where they have a voice that is heard. And kids need to have a lot of say-so in what goes on in their life through their preschool and grade school years. Then they can enter their teen years more relaxed and less rebellious. They know how to ask for what they want in respectful ways that work. Parents will avoid the high intensity power struggles that so many parents are waging with their teens today, at a time when the parents naturally have less and less control.

This process that works so well to gain cooperation in the mornings, after preschool, and at bedtime for young children will work just as well for issues such as homework, TV time, phone time, and curfews. Kids will also have learned the meaning of accountability, so it becomes just a matter of keep doing what you've been doing over the years.

And if you think it was hard to "detach and let go" with

your tantrumming three year old, wait until you get to your headstrong 17-year-old with definite plans for prom night! But it's not that hard if you've built up a full Goodwill Account. And it's not that hard if you and your teen have had years of experience in sitting down and talking over these kinds of issues, hearing each other's concerns, and creating clear, win-win agreements. And it's not that hard if you trust yourself to follow through on these agreements. And if you've seen your kids be responsible for themselves and their decisions over many years, and seen that they usually make good decisions, it really is much easier to let go and trust them making choices and decisions as teenagers.

TIME FOR WHAT'S REALLY IMPORTANT

When you take the time up front, preventatively, to avoid all the frustrating, tiresome power struggles, peace and calm will reign in your home. It will just feel more peaceful, more fun.

Imagine for a moment that every morning your kids wake up; get dressed on their own without any complaints; handle their bathroom duties; come to the breakfast table with enough time for everyone to have a nutritious meal together; make their lunches and gather their schoolwork on their own; everyone leaves on time and happy; the car ride to school is fun and full of lively conversation; the good-bye's at school are warm and brief; you pull out of the school parking lot feeling secure that your kids are happy and in the right place for their needs; and finally you arrive at work a few minutes early ready and willing for your workday to begin. Then after work, you arrive at the school eager to see your kids. You walk into the preschool with the expectation that because your morning was so calm and peaceful, that your child had a great day. They run up and hug you and then show you off to their friends. After playing a few minutes, they want to go home. You hold hands out to the car, and all the way home you sing songs with your favorite tape. On arrival home, you quickly put on your play clothes and join your kids outside for some fun. A half an hour later you start dinner, with your preschooler joining you in the cooking process.

After dinner, the family spends some time playing together outside before it's time for baths. They come inside without a fight because of the choices you gave them earlier. Soon they are in your lap reading their favorite books. After singing your favorite nursery rhymes together, making a few blanket forts, and saying prayers, you snuggle for a while as you tell each other your happiest and saddest moments of the day. One last hug and you leave their room right on time with your bedtime agreement. You and your spouse then have some time to talk about your day, wrapped around some quiet personal time. And when you turn out the lights on your day, you fall asleep feeling like your life is working; like you've struck a healthy balance between home and work. You feel a sense of pride and accomplishment in both your parenting life and your work life.

Sound impossible? It's not. You have to invest some time and energy up front to prepare yourself and your kids for a change of discipline models. And there usually is a little "hump" you have to get through for several weeks as you switch the model for how your home works. Some kids will throw the book at you to try to get you sucked back into the old games and the old way they used to get their sense of power and control.

And thus come some moments of truth, when your will and resolve will be tested. You won't be in a battle of wills like you were in the past. This is a test for how well you can stay disciplined. Disciplined not to argue, remind, yell, and overpower. To not go back to the old games. And if you persist and follow through without the fuss and mess, your kids will pretty quickly feel your new resolve and they'll let go of the pushing and struggles. Kids can sense a wishy-washy adult a mile away, and that's the person they will push buttons with. And, they also can sense when an adult means what they say, because there is a firmness in their attitude, tone of voice, and body language. And kids respond to those adults with cooperation and respect.

So stick with it. Hang in there and get through the initial transition period. Once you've handled one area, then subsequent issues will be handled much more easily because everyone is on the same page about the new way things are handled in your home. It really will get much easier. And if you have regular weekly family meetings, you have a process to fine tune any problem areas and smooth out the rough edges. Which is much easier than dealing with daily power struggles that feel more like crisis management and damage control.

Best of luck to you and your family. I hope this book will help you create more time for the spontaneous fun and play that many families miss out on today because of overbooked schedules and too much time wasted on power struggles.

One of my favorite quotes is by Mother Theresa. "Everyone today seems to be in such a terrible rush. Anxious for greater riches and greater developments and so on. So that kids have very little time with their parents. And parents have very little time with each other. And so in the home begins the disruption of the peace of the world."

When you create in your homes what I know you can create by using what you've learned in this book, you will be adding your contribution to the peace of the world.

Bibliography

Bluestein, Jane. *21st Century Discipline*, Health Communications, 1995.

Brazelton, T. Berry. *Touchpoints: Your Child's Emotional and Behavioral Development*, Addison Wesley, 1992.

Brazelton, T. Berry and Stanley Greenspan. *The Irreducible Needs of Children*, Perseus Publishing, 2000.

Covey, Stephen. *The Seven Habits of Highly Effective Families*, Golden Books, 1997.

Dreikers, Rudolph. *Children the Challenge*, Hawthorn Books, 1964.

Fraiberg, Selma. *The Magic Years*, Scribner's Sons, 1959.

Jordan, Tim. *What I Learned at Summer Camp: About Understanding and Loving Our Children*, St. Louis Youth Camps Press, 1994.

Jordan, Tim and Sally Rains. *Keeping Your Kids Grounded When*

Bibliography

You're Flying by the Seat of Your Pants, Palmerston and Reed, 1999.

Kvols, Kathryn. *Redirecting Children's Behavior*, Parenting Press, Inc., 1998.

Nelson, Jane. *Positive Discipline*, Ballantine Books, 1987.

Neville, Helen and Diane Clark Johnson. *Temperament Tools: Working with Your Child's Inborn Traits*, Parenting Press, 1997.

Additional Resources

Families First Parenting Series:

Solving Your Child's Sleeping Problems: A Guide For Tired Parents™, audiocassette by Tim Jordan, M.D.

I Gotta Be Me: Helping Your Children Be All They Can Be™, audiocassette by Tim Jordan, M.D.

Rise and Shine: Redirecting Everyday Power Struggles™, audiocassette by Tim Jordan, M.D.

Ain't Misbehavin': Understanding the Ups and Downs of Early Childhood™, audiocassette by Tim Jordan, M.D.

Teens Rock! Understanding and Loving Your Teenager™, audiocassette by Tim Jordan, M.D.

International Network for Children and Families: Provides positive parenting courses and instructor training for the "Redirecting Children's Behavior" classes throughout the U.S. and abroad. For information call 1-800-277-6651.

Additional Resources

For more information on Dr. Jordan's retreats and camps for kids and teens, training courses for professionals, his parenting products, or to learn more about his availability as a keynote or workshop presenter call 636-530-1883, or visit his Web site at www.timjordanmd.com.